eye on society

Addicts

Drugs and alcohol re-examined

A young barbiturate-injector loses consciousness before he has time to withdraw the syringe

Addicts

Drugs and alcohol re-examined

JAMES WILLIS
MB, FRCP (Edin), MRC Psych

Pitman Publishing

First published 1973

Sir Isaac Pitman and Sons Ltd
Pitman House, Parker Street, Kingsway, London WC2B 5PB
PO Box 46038, Portal Street, Nairobi, Kenya
Sir Isaac Pitman (Aust) Pty Ltd
Pitman House, 158 Bouverie Street, Carlton, Victoria 3053, Australia
Pitman Publishing Company SA Ltd
PO Box No 11231, Johannesburg, South Africa
Pitman Publishing Corporation
6 East 43rd Street, New York, NY 10017, USA
Sir Isaac Pitman (Canada) Ltd
495 Wellington Street West, Toronto 135, Canada
The Copp Clark Publishing Company
517 Wellington Street West, Toronto 135, Canada

ISBN: 0 273 36031 0

Set in 11 on 12pt IBM Baskerville, printed by photolithography, and bound in Great Britain at The Pitman Press, Bath

G 4640:18

Preface

I have been invited to write a short book about the misuse of drugs and alcohol for a more general readership than that to which a traditional textbook or work of reference is suited. I have tried to do this with such readers in mind, avoiding the sort of jargon that we doctors know and love. I have also specifically omitted references to tobacco and nicotine since I do not have the necessary expertise to deal properly with the history of its use and undoubted harmful effects. As a psychiatrist much of my professional experience and interest lies in the abuse of drugs and alcohol.

As far as possible I have avoided discussing the technicalities of the substances involved, as I believe that the social and personal aspects of substance abuse are far more relevant to the present inquiry.

There is one term which occurs frequently throughout the book and that may cause difficulty to some readers, namely "control." This term will be found in such phrases as "control subjects" or "control series." It means that the individuals who compose the "control groups" have been selected for the specific purpose of being compared with drug-users or alcohol-users, while they themselves are not drug- or alcohol-users.

J.W.

Acknowledgements

The author and publisher would like to thank the following for permission to use the illustrations in this book, the page numbers of which appear below:

David Bush: Frontispiece, 70, 100, 110, 147, 152
Camera Press: 2, 50, 119, 135, 176, 177, 180
Ciba-Zeitschrift: 39
Daily Telegraph Colour Library: 157, 161
Mark Edwards: 7, 32, 43
Larry Herman: 5, 10, 121, 163, 169
Archie Hill: 13
Peter Moeschlin: 20
H. Newport-Gwilt: 84
Radio Times Hulton Picture Library: 80
Syndication Internationale: 173, 174
The Ulster Folk Museum: 125
The Victoria and Albert Museum: 34
The Wellcome Trustees: 33, 40
World Health Organization: 55, 68, 72, 106

Care has been taken to obtain permission where appropriate, but should there be any case in which this has inadvertently been neglected the authors and publisher apologise sincerely for the omission.

for M

Contents

Chapter 1

General introduction

In recent years many of the problems of drug-misuse have made an impact on the attention of the public and have caused national and international concern. But for many hundreds of years, even as far back as 2000 BC we find references to man's tendency to employ self-intoxication as a way of releasing himself from care and of insulating himself against the miseries of his existence. Nevertheless, it is mainly in the past three hundred years that we find real evidence of widespread alcohol and drug abuse as constituting serious social problems.

In this work it is the writer's intention to show that substance-misuse on a large scale is not so much a new problem as one which has intensified with technological advances and which seems to have grown more prevalent as man's social conditions have become more complicated.

It is, of course, apparent that no matter what legal or social constraints may operate, people are usually able to find ways of intoxicating themselves, in the short or in the long term. They will often do this for personal gratification, either to alleviate the misery that is forced on them through social conditions or when quite by chance, they find that a drug or other substance makes them feel good. Fashion, too, and modish behaviour will frequently influence people to use alcohol and drugs.

Substance-abuse may therefore be viewed as symptomatic of personal illness or of social disorder. At present drug-misuse is being given a great deal of public attention, but we should realize that by sheer weight of numbers the misuse of alcohol leads the field and that alcoholism is a prime threat to public health, often entailing disastrous personal and social consequences.

WHAT IS A DRUG? WHAT IS ADDICTION?

The World Health Organization (1969) defines a drug as "any substance that, when taken into the living organism, may modify

Fashion and modish behaviour may influence people to use alcohol and drugs (Scene from the "Legalize Pot" Rally, 1968)

one or more of its functions." This straightforward definition gives us a starting-point in our examination of the special problems which include drugs of many sorts but which will centre on their use and abuse by man for reasons outside what is strictly medical. Clearly the World Health Organization in its definition of a drug gives us a wide frame of reference, for the term drug covers an enormous range of substances – from simple pain-relieving drugs, such as aspirin, to vitamin preparations, and ultimately to the more sophisticated preparations that are used in the treatment of severe and complicated infections, metabolic disturbances and the like, which, until the last thirty years, were virtually untreatable. For the purpose of our discussions the drugs to which we refer are those drugs which may be abused or misused because they have a specific effect on a person's mental state. The abuse relates to the subjective effects on the individual when he takes the drug. Such experiences may be first of all pleasurable, ranging from a calming effect to a state of stimulation or excitement and to disruptive states in which a person's perceptions of the world around him are disorganized and changed.

National and worldwide concern centres on the increase of casual self-intoxication by means of a wide range of drugs on the part of an expanding and apparently increasingly youthful population. The areas of drug-abuse which have caused the most concern are those which involve dependency-producing drugs (dependence or addiction being a state in which a person is unable to stop taking a substance because of strong physical, psychological, and social reasons).

What is addiction? What is dependence? These are questions that are frequently asked. Again the World Health Organization (1969) provides a good working definition:

"Drug-dependence is a state, psychic and sometimes also physical, resulting from the interaction between a living organism and a drug, characterized by behavioural and other responses that always include a compulsion to take the drugs on a continuous or periodic basis in order to experience its psychic effects, and sometimes to avoid the discomfort of its absence. Tolerance may or may not be present. A person may be dependent on more than one drug."

Now this definition is formal and concise since it is designed by international agreement to meet the needs of scientific and social inquiry. Although it meets the requirements of specialists very satisfactorily, for the general reader some elaboration is necessary.

Reference has already been made to the use of the word drug in the context of drug-abuse and drug-dependence. It should be emphasized that in the areas covered by this book, reference will frequently be made to the effect of certain drugs on human behaviour, on feeling, awareness of the world, and on thinking; in short on the higher mental functions. For many drugs which affect people in these areas are not only capable of producing states of dependence but are also the more likely to be abused. This brings us to another term that needs to be clarified, namely *drug-abuse.*

The World Health Organization (1969) defines drug-abuse as "persistent or sporadic excessive drug-use inconsistent with or unrelated to acceptable medical practice." This again is a reasonable definition.

It will be useful to bear these terms in mind, for they will be reiterated in this book, and it is essential that their meaning be clearly understood. However, it should be realized that to confine our attention merely to substances that have primary medical uses is too narrow an area of concern since man frequently takes substances which have no medical uses at all, alcohol and tobacco being the obvious examples.

In taking such substances people have sought to alter their feelings. They have generally been motivated by their search for pleasure, but they have had other reasons, too, that may be connected with their psychological make-up, their fears and anxieties, their need to participate in social activities. Such activities may have a religious setting or they may range from week-end beer-drinking at a Rugby club to campus "pot"-smoking.

The drug scene today owes its significance not just to the increase in drug-abuse and drug-dependence, with their social consequences, but also to the scientific revolution in medicine of the last fifty years. As a result an increasing variety of highly potent substances has been made available. Many of these substances act with great benefit but their existence involves possible dangers, and there must be an awareness of the responsibilities that go with their use.

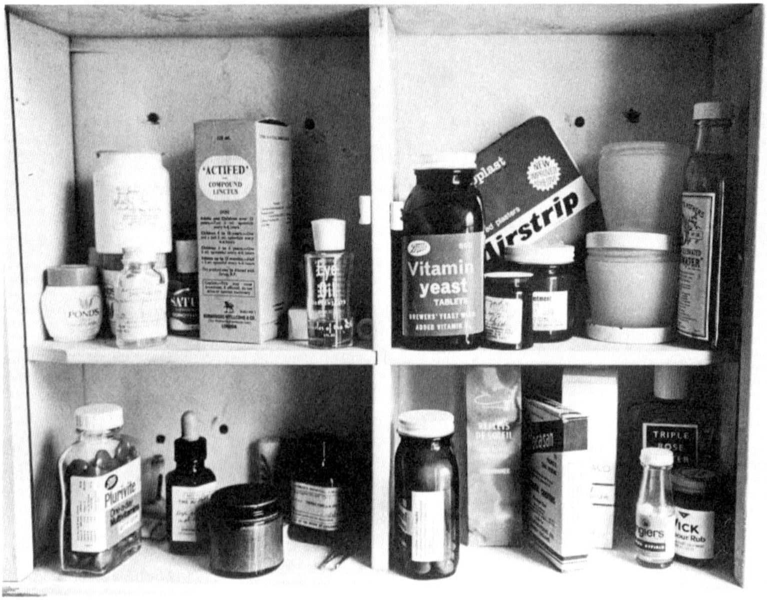

This is a pill-oriented age. Everyone's medicine cupboard contains drugs of some kind

It is frequently said that this is a "pill-oriented" age and that people too easily take tablets or pills to make them feel happier, calmer and more cheerful. This is no doubt true; people are less wary of taking medicines prescribed for them by doctors, but they are hardly to be blamed for this. It seems that a whole generation has been educated by the doctors to expect relief from all sorts of symptoms and diseases, and it is natural that they should go to them and ask for help. It is with the misuse of all the varieties of substances and alcohol that this book is mainly concerned. It is in no sense a technical work; rather it is intended to be a provocative stimulus to the real intellectual curiosity which the public should have. This is essential if any real progress is to be made in the appreciation of the causation and treatment of the disorders that go with alcohol and drug-misuse.

But this is not the end of the problem, for we also need to look at the larger picture – namely that of drug-use in its widest possible context. There is a hypothesis, as yet unproven, that we are witnessing a significant historical and social change; that western society may be turning more and more to drug-use in a casual way, heedless of its possible dangers, and is establishing the practice as a new and forceful element in cultural change. Only the future will show whether or not this hypothesis is correct. Meanwhile, there is need for a full discussion of those facts we know about drugs while, at the same time, removing the myths and fantasies that often surround them. It is also necessary to look at the prejudices and irrational attitudes that may materially influence public policy; in short we have to examine the meaning and significance of the situation as a whole.

THE NATURE OF DEPENDENCE – PHYSICAL, PSYCHIC OR BOTH?

It may well be that attempts to distinguish between physical and psychological dependence are too elaborate; however, since the terms are in current use it is necessary to know how they are used.

Physical dependence refers to states in which a definite biological change is thought to take place in the body following drug-taking. This change initiates a physical need to continue taking the drug. It may not be permanent; indeed, it is more likely to be transient, but it will be sufficiently intense to cause someone to continue with the drug in order to avoid distressing symptoms – sometimes very dangerous symptoms, such as the fits which occur during withdrawal from barbiturates. These symptoms, too, have a physical basis, that is, they affect the very cells of the body.

Psychological dependence refers to emotional drives and needs which make a person continue taking the drug even though he does not experience a physical craving. This psychological dependence arises in the first place from the wish to repeat a pleasant drug-induced experience, and for most users this is the primary attraction of dependence. However, drug-use also has the ability to banish unpleasant feelings, fears, and anxieties, to relieve gloom and despair and ultimately to produce a shield between a person and the unacceptable realities of his life.

Under the influence of drugs a person's pattern of behaviour will frequently change. The user's emotional needs and drives will be affected by the drug. Fear of being without drugs will also

Alienation caused through psychological dependence? Or vice versa?

influence his behaviour. These changes do not extend only to the user; they affect other members of society too, for drug-taking is not just a personal matter. It inevitably brings in its train social consequences of a far-reaching nature.

It is naive to assert, as people sometimes do, that drug-usage is merely a matter for individual choice. Such an assertion takes a very egocentric view of human behaviour. There can be few people in the world who are so socially isolated that their behaviour does not impinge on others in some way. A parallel may be drawn here between drug use and suicide. It is often said that suicide only concerns the individual himself. In the final analysis this is true only for a small number of extremely isolated people.

The changes in behaviour that follow psychic dependence are fairly subtle. When a person is dependent on a drug his whole social identity may alter, not because of the effects of the drug but because of the attitudes that society has towards that drug. If it is a drug that society views unfavourably the taker is quite likely to cut himself off from others, to be drawn more and more into the company of other drug-users and to identify with them as a group amongst whom he feels safer and more readily accepted. He may then take on a new identity. Since drug-use is so commonly a shared experience of the group and since it is disowned by society, the user sometimes sees himself as alienated from society because he is despised by it. More and more he adopts the values and ideas of his fellow drug-users who also see themselves as a special group and develop their own customs, morals and language. In short they develop the beginnings of a culture all of their own – a subculture in which they share a common social identity.

"DRUG" – A DIFFICULT WORD

Another difficulty arises from the very word "drug." For many people a drug means something that makes them sleepy, that "weakens the will"; it is something they tend to equate with the vague notion of being "drugged." This is connected with a numbe of factors, including perhaps the influence of fiction where innocent girls are drugged by seducers and kidnappers, and where victims are drugged so that they will reveal secrets. It may also be linked with the fantasies and myths that people have about the effect of drugs on sexual behaviour. In this context recruits to the armed services have frequently believed that "bromide" was put into the tea to dampen their sexual desires during rigorous training. Again, in the Second World War propagandists advised servicemen not to take antimalarial tablets in case they caused sexual impotence. These examples make one realize that people's fears about drugs may be a curious mixture of half-truth, myth and fantasy. Thus when a worried patient asks "Is it a drug, doctor?" his simple question may conceal considerable anxiety and misgiving.

People may well be worried by the common fear of loss of consciousness, of loss of self-control, of being influenced by the will of someone else. This fear of being controlled, of not being completely in command of oneself, often finds expression in the simple remark of a normal person, "I am under drugs." In its most extreme form it is seen in some people with severe mental illnesses such as schizophrenia. Such people may develop the notion that they are being poisoned by drugs administered by sinister unseen persecutors with the object of gaining control over them, of influencing them and directing them.

THE DRUG-PEDDLER

The person who sells drugs to addicts for personal gain and who is not himself an addict is rightly regarded by society as a menace. Nevertheless, it is important to try to keep a cool head when looking at this variety of antisocial behaviour. Prison sentences and strong sanctions are likely to act as a deterrent. Meanwhile the extent of the drug-peddler's activities must not be distorted through understandable fears that society has about such people.

In the United Kingdom the illicit selling of "hard" drugs has so far been from one addict to another. There is very little evidence of "pushing" by non-addicted people for monetary gain. However, there is evidence that "soft" drugs (stimulants and drugs such as LSD) are sold by non-users purely for profit. In the United States professional drug-selling involves an elaborate chain of distribution, with importers at the top who are not themselves drug-users. The importers arrange for the adulteration

In Britain addicts sometimes sell drugs to other addicts, especially in certain recognized areas in the larger cities

of the drugs, which are then passed down a chain of distributors at street-level. Rewards at each level involve either money or drugs or both.

Society's negative attitudes towards sellers can sometimes obscure the situation and hamper the development of treatment agencies. It is assumed, for instance, that drug-sellers will automatically flock to areas around clinics and hospitals. When New York State first started drug-dependence treatment programmes it was widely asserted that peddlers would congregate around state hospitals and other institutions where addicts were being treated. Yet this never happened, for drug-peddlers are not so naive as to invite arrest so easily; they never have done so and they are never likely to.

ARE ALCOHOLISM AND DRUG-DEPENDENCE ILLNESSES?

This is a fundamental question and one that cannot be shirked. When human behaviour persistently offends the susceptibilities of society it becomes necessary to find some explanation. In Western society there is a general belief that man is responsible for his actions and must bear responsibility for their consequences. This rather shaky assumption may have simple consequences. If someone persistently behaves contrary to the norms of society he may be categorized along a "good . . . bad" baseline and his behaviour may then be explained in terms of his position along a "goodness . . . badness" continuum. Thus people who are frequent offenders will be regarded as "very bad," in contrast to less frequent or "once-only" offenders. The "very bad" person may be regarded as being of "weak character" or of "low moral fibre" and there the matter may rest. But this is an over-simplification and does not account for all the vagaries of human behaviour.

In practice, when society is faced with persistent offenders, whose abnormalities of conduct start early and continue throughout adult life, it tends to react, as it has so often done in the past, by asserting that such people must be ill; their conduct can only be explained by presupposing some form of psychological illness or some basic flaw in their make-up. This suggestion is usually put forward because persistently abnormal conduct does not respond to conventional forms of punishment. "If he's so bad that punishment doesn't reform him he must be ill."

Dictionary definitions of health and illness tend to stress the presence of one in the absence of the other and official definitions, of such terms as "mental illness" or "mental health" tend to be tenuous and unhelpful. Bewley (1970) has commented on the difficulty of defining terms such as drug-dependence in terms of illness. It is agreed that there are semantic difficulties involved in defining drug-dependence or alcoholism entirely as illnesses. On the other hand it is equally agreed that regarding these two varieties of human behaviour as illnesses is a humane beginning to our understanding them. Perhaps the North-European puritan tradition contributes to our difficulty in all this. Yolles (1970) has commented that much of the rather rigid public attitude towards drug abuse present in America for many years may well be traced to the puritan attitudes brought to America by the early settlers from the United Kingdom who took with them less of the *laissez-faire* hedonism of Charles I and a good deal more of the puritanism of their religious teachers.

It may be thought that the discussion of these points is merely an academic quibble but such a criticism would be less than fair. We must have some clear ideas about the meanings of the terms we use, and while pragmatic and humane considerations may urge us to interpret drug-abuse and alcoholism as forms of sickness such an interpretation may be as over-simplified as regarding both as vice – based on inherent human badness. One difficulty is that our concept of illness is extremely vague indeed, the concept of "mental illness" is constantly under review. At one time the "mentally ill" used to receive "custodial treatment" in asylums or prisons when they broke the laws. With the increase in awareness of the complexities of human behaviour it has become the practice of behavioural scientists to categorize behaviour in a more rational way, so that the sick may be treated and the wicked punished. Yet we need not flatter ourselves that our categorizations are particularly expert. The decision to give a prisoner psychiatric treatment may be quite arbitrary, even fortuitous, and honest psychiatrists are soon made aware of their limitations when they enter prison work. At the same time hospitals find themselves confronted with serious problems in the care of offenders regarded as ill. Thus when we regard the offender as "ill" this is very often a matter of convenience stemming from humanitarian principles. It may be helpful but does not provide a complete explanation. There are serious gaps in our knowledge and fundamental dilemmas remain unresolved. A person who consults a psychiatrist is not necessarily suffering from a psychiatric or mental illness just because he has entered the psychiatrist's office. Indeed, in recent years there has been a move among psychiatrists to cast doubt on the reliability of their own psychiatric diagnosis, and in some instances to question their value at all!

But to return to drug-dependence and alcoholism, one is perhaps on surer ground here because the people involved with these substances often develop physical and psychiatric complications. Drug effects can look like psychiatric disorders or they can actually trigger them off. Alcohol can cause not only deterioration of a person's total mode of behaviour but also permanent brain-damage of a progressive sort (dementia) as well as transient psychoses, for example, delirium tremens.

Here are concrete examples of illness about which no one would disagree. It is likely that the association of alcoholism and drug-use with disease arose because physicians became aware of their consequences to health. They then reasoned that someone who became involved with these substances was more likely to be ill than not. Even if this reasoning is not one hundred per cent cogent it does reflect a humanitarian and a sensible approach to the study of human behaviour. The pragmatic approach is an important feature of medical practice today. It is not many centuries since madmen were regarded as evil and subjected to torture and punishment. Less than seven centuries ago epileptics were buried alive in Scotland.

We might summarize by saying that the concept of mental illness takes as its starting-point the inability of an individual

Apathy, if nothing worse, can be the result of the bottle

to function normally or to consider the extent of the handicap from which he suffers. Changes in his behaviour may be manifested in terms of personal, physical, and social implications.

At a more sophisticated level one would take into account the effects of the "illness" on the family, especially if it destroys the relationships within the family, and if it affects the individuals performance in the world at a professional, social and interpersonal level.

Thus to regard dependence on alcohol and on drugs as a kind of disease does constitute a humane and a practical approach in our efforts to understand a very complex area of human behaviour. It should also be added that in general people are more inclined to regard alcoholism and drug-dependence as illnesses in their own right rather than to consider them as varieties of deviant behaviour – such as stealing, for example. Drug-addicts and alcoholics are, after all, continuously damaging themselves with toxic substances, and to act in this way is, to say the least, an abnormal way of carrying on. On the other hand, one might ask whether smoking should be regarded as an illness, or, for that matter, excessive gambling. To pose such questions shows that the problem is really very complicated.

WHAT IS SUBJECTIVE?

One of the most difficult problems in understanding how it is that people become dependent on a drug lies in the fact that there is really no way of describing the drug-taker's mental experiences. It is easy enough to observe and measure physical changes – for instance alterations in the pulse-rate, blood-pressure, breathing-rate and, when necessary, to institute such refined investigations as recording the electrical activity of the brain (electroencephalogram). However, this tells us very little about the individual's subjective experience, and we are left with the problem of being able to study physical effects of a substance but of having no way of appreciating the subjective psychic effects. Nevertheless, for very many drug-users it is the basic psychic experience which, initially at least, produces a state of drug-dependence. It is true that the pleasurable subjective effects may not persist (and this may lead the individual to try other drugs) but initially, at least, the subjective pleasure is a powerful motivating and reinforcing agent.

This leads us to consider one of the most crucial issues in psychological and psychiatric investigation, namely the nature of the mind/body relationship (psyche/soma). Now these are problems which have engaged man's curiosity and thinking for many centuries. Is the mind independent of the brain? Is the brain the organic basis of the mind? No doubt semantic difficulties are relevant to these questions, but such an observation does not solve the problem.

Philosophical theories tend to dominate the discussion of these questions, so that one is left with the choice of selecting between the explanations offered by scholars such as Aristotle and Aquinas who saw human behaviour as governed by monism, a doctrine which assumes an essential unity of body and mind, or the dualism of Descartes who viewed the concepts "mental" and "physical" as almost belonging to two distinct watertight compartments. Then there is the existentialist viewpoint which regards the subjectivity of psychological experience as of primary significance. These are scholarly issues of great importance, and they underlie many of the divisions that exist in psychological investigation and in the psychiatric approach to normal and abnormal human behaviour.

Thus one school may view all mental activity as having what is basically a biochemically-determined origin, probably influenced more by inheritance than by environment, whilst another may lay stress on the effects of a person's early infantile experience and his subsequent subjective psychic experience. But whatever viewpoint is taken, our real understanding of these problems is surely confused and often based on assertions that have not yet been verified. The situation becomes more complicated when one comes to consider the effects of drugs and alcohol and the reasons that impel people to abuse them. We might expect the question to yield a simple answer: we have an individual; we then identify the type of drug or alcohol and measure many of their physical and some of their psychological effects; the subject can be observed, interviewed and so on – before, during, and after the effects. Yet our ignorance about the subjective nature of the human experience remains. All we have is our observation of the individual's actions and reactions.

To be sure, we know that people with damaged brains show recognizable changes in behaviour, intellectual impairment, loss of memory concerning recent events, loss of the sense of orientation for time and place, but the extent of these observed changes does not necessarily correlate with the actual extent of structural brain-damage. In fact serious brain-damage may be combined with minimal mental disturbance, while people with major "mental" disturbances such as schizophrenia often show no apparent brain-abnormality. The position is even more complicated when we realize that many drugs can produce states of mental disturbance which resemble well-recognized psychiatric disorders. This can happen with amphetamines (Connell, 1957). Further, a wide range of drugs – from aspirin to steroids – can cause states of delirium, that is, excited over-activity in a state of altered consciousness. This finding may be regarded as tantalizing, although it could throw light on the relationship between brain and mind.

SUMMARY

We have considered the general notion of dependence and abuse, the idea that dependence involves disease and the suspicion that psychological phenomena are hard to explain. We shall now go on to examine briefly some of the substances concerned.

Chapter 2

Drugs and their effects

GENERAL OBSERVATIONS

Perhaps one of the most dangerous assumptions made about the effects of drugs and alcohol is that the effects frequently described in particular cases will necessarily be common to all other cases. In fact effects may differ considerably from case to case.

The pharmacologist who has made a careful study of the nature of drug action and its effects on animals and human beings is far from certain in his pronouncements and predictions. This is especially true of drugs which alter mental processes. Here results from experiments often diverge considerably from popular notions about drugs that have, to a large extent, been fostered by emotionally charged statements issuing from the mass media.

Any consideration of the effects on the mental state and behaviour of a person must always include a careful contemporary evaluation of that person, the setting in which he took the drug, his expectations of its effects and the expectations of those, if any, observing him. This area of study is complicated by the fact that many drugs are actually classified according to their predominant effects; yet it is far from certain that the pharmacological action will follow a particular pattern. Take for example, the stimulant effect of amphetamine drugs. It is true that in general they stimulate, but in the case of a small proportion of people the effect is a calming one. This is specially true of certain hyperkinetic (over active) children and a minority of explosive assaultative people whose disordered behaviour is regarded as psychopathic. Another example is that of the most widely used sleeping-pills, the barbiturates. It is generally agreed that these are sedative since their main action is to depress brain activity. But before this effect occurs they often excite people and reduce inhibitions.

A person taking sleeping-tablets may sleep more easily and soundly with their help, but he may just as easily go to sleep with the non-sedative tranquillizers. Should he happen to try "sedative" tablets in a different setting he is likely to experience or become aware of a different effect. A typical example of this would be the not uncommon case of the person who discovers by accident that the initial barbiturate effect is one of mild stimulation like that of alcohol. This initial effect, usually lasting for about thirty to forty minutes, depending on the barbiturate taken, is one in which the person is made more talkative by reason of the lowering of anxiety, more cheerful and in general less inhibited. This has proved to be the case where someone has found that taking barbiturates before a party produces a state very similar to that of alcoholic intoxication, whereas if these tablets were taken at night he would go calmly to sleep.

The same is true of stimulant-type drugs, though to a lesser extent. Stimulants *do* make people feel more awake and alert, but as their effect wears off drowsiness can occur. Conversely, there are a few people who experience the opposite effect with stimulants, and become calmer and even drowsy under their effect. In clinical practice it is not uncommon to find patients who have transferred their dependence from one substance to another, often by chance. One example was of a thirty-eight-year-old man who was referred to a clinic for investigation of severe dependence on barbiturates. His past history revealed that until five years previously he had been heavily dependent on alcohol and had twice been admitted to hospital for treatment for alcoholism. One day when he had insufficient money to buy drink he took some sleeping-pills which had been prescribed for him by his doctor and in taking them by day he found that they produced in him feelings just like those of alcoholic intoxication. Within the next few weeks he became heavily dependent on barbiturates.

When one looks at the consequences of using the more powerful mind-altering drugs the position becomes even more confused. From time to time public statements are made about the supposed effects of drugs and their relation to various criminal acts, and their connection with suicide. In the past a number of claims have been made about the supposed effects of cannabis and its part in causing excited and anti-social behaviour; yet firm evidence to support such claims is extremely slender. Certainly the history of the whole problem suggests that particular substances tend to acquire a magical reputation. It is almost as if the fact that their effects are unknown impels people to speculate about them and to weave fantasies around them.

It has been suggested that amphetamines may contribute to road accidents caused by lack of judgement by lorry-drivers who take them to keep awake. However, surveys in the United States lend no support to the theory. In fact the main group of drugs that appears to produce consistent errors of judgement while driving is the tranquillizers (and these are not usually regarded as drugs of abuse). The place of alcohol in traffic accidents is, of course, much more clearly defined. Tranquillizers, on the other hand, are less likely to be regarded as substances of abuse since they are given under medical supervision, but the fact that a drug is given under medical supervision does not confer on the user an automatic exclusion from the possibility of social hazards in its use.

It is almost as if drugs are divided into *dangerous* and *non-dangerous* kinds, purely on the basis of whether they are prescribed by doctors. This is a risky assumption. Aspirin, many pain-relievers, hay-fever remedies (antihistamines), tranquillizers, some antidepressants – all these can alter consciousness quite considerably. Drugs taken for "pleasure," that is not prescribed, tend to be regarded as dangerous, but even an examination of "pleasure" induced by drugs in the experimental situation yields conflicting results. Thus the assumption is, to say the least, shaky. For instance the opiates are said to be supremely pleasure-giving. Yet an experimental study into their subjective effects yielded far less certain results than was the case with barbiturates and amphetamines. Only a small percentage – about 30 per cent – reported opiates as pleasurable, as opposed to 70 per cent of the same group who reported amphetamines as consistently so.

Categorizing drug effects on the basis of their use in medical or non-medical settings is likely to be misleading. A person is not excluded from risk just because his drugs are prescribed for him. He may not break the Drug Laws but he can err in other

The cat has been given a dose of LSD. When confronted with the mouse it first reacted normally, advancing with ears flattened and pupils dilated. It then suddenly retreated in confusion and apparent fear

ways. In the words of Blum, "Drugs may modify behaviour but they do not create it."

It is for these reasons that the main attention needs to be focused on the individual himself who takes the drug and on his environment, rather than merely on the drug itself.

Another example of the misconceptions that can surround drug-use is in the area of the action of hallucinogens. LSD is regarded by many as being mainly hallucinogenic in action. In fact experiments with LSD in an experimental setting suggest that the hallucinatory effect is by no means primary. Perhaps it is the intensely dramatic nature of a hallucinatory experience that caused the drug to be labelled as primarily hallucinogenic. This again indicates that a great deal of what seems to be real knowledge about the effects of drugs is cloudy and tends to be linked to pronouncements made by the non-scientific. These pronouncements tend to get repeated throughout the literature on drugs without any tests or experiments being carried out. An attitude of cautious and informed scepticism needs to be encouraged.

In the field of treatment involving mind-altering drugs there are recurrent examples of this. Since 1957 there have been available to doctors an increasing range of *antidepressant* drugs. These are powerful substances which appear to cause remission of states of pathological depression and the drugs involved are widely used. Yet examination of their usefulness brings one to a contentious area. Early reports have, on the whole, been more enthusiastic than later ones, and when properly controlled clinical trials are used the effectiveness of antidepressants becomes less certain and clear. Now if these difficulties arise in situations where drug action can be observed and monitored, that is in treatment, it should be realized that the whole area of the effects of drugs on behaviour is even more uncertain, especially when these drugs are taken casually.

An instructive example relates to a man of twenty-four who was referred to a clinic because of severe amphetamine dependence. He had a bad record of delinquent behaviour and aggression, and had frequently been in prison. It was agreed that he was an antisocial psychopath – a person with virtually no control over antisocial tendencies which had been present since early childhood. At seventeen he became involved in amphetamines and said that they helped him to feel calmer and that they damped down his aggressive impulses. Now it is a fact that there is a minority of aggresive psychopaths whose explosive behaviour is paradoxically modified by amphetamines. Possibly this individual stumbled on the discovery by chance; certainly there is no evidence to suggest that he had read about it. He was a demanding, immature person who angrily asked for large quantities of amphetamines "to stop myself from getting into trouble." It was suggested to him that his life-history was such that one could expect, if not predict, further episodes of violent behaviour and that his apparent needs might be better served by admission to hospital and a full examination, but he angrily dismissed the proposal. He said "I'll worry about the next time when it happens." Within the next two weeks he was again in custody and received a long sentence for murder. Under the influence of amphetamines, which had been illicitly obtained he had exploded again into violence and had become excited and uncontrolled.

The question to be asked is whether he belonged to that minority group of aggressive psychopaths who are calmed by amphetamines. This is not certain, but the story is cited to show how difficult it is to examine the relationship between antisocial behaviour produced by drugs and antisocial behaviour originating in a basically disturbed aggressive personality. This is an extreme example, no doubt, but extreme examples are important reminders of the complexity of the issues involved.

To sum up then, the main attention needs to be focused on the individual himself who takes a drug and on his environment, rather than merely on the drug itself.

THE SUBSTANCES INVOLVED

In this section we shall be describing the patterns of dependence associated with various substances. Some mention will also be made of the substances themselves with a brief account of their actions and medical uses. Of course this is not to be regarded in any sense as more than an outline since a comprehensive survey would fall outside the scope of this work. The pharmacology – that is to say the chemical structure and mode of action of the substances – is properly the concern of a

Piranesi's "Carceri d'invenzione" (an imaginary prison) painted in the eighteenth century. Coleridge regarded this as a true representation of an opium-induced vision.

scientific inquiry, so that even a shortened account could mislead. Interested readers are directed to standard works on the subject, a list of which appears at the end of the book.

A convenient way of grouping the substances can be made under the following three headings:

1 Drugs which have an action which is predominantly sedative,
2 Drugs which have an action which is predominantly stimulant
3 Drugs which have a hallucinogenic action.

1 SEDATIVE DRUGS

For practical purposes these may be considered under two headings:

A. Narcotic analgesics, that is drugs which have a powerful pain-relieving action and which also produce alterations in consciousness, especially drowsiness.
B. The sedative drugs, including barbiturates and barbiturate-like sedatives. These are, in general, drugs used to promote sleep and also to produce mild states of day-time sedation.

(a) The Narcotic Analgesics.

Of all the drugs encountered in the field of dependence, these are the drugs which, above all, possess the most intensive dependency-producing potential. The list of such drugs is large indeed and includes not only the opiates, that is drugs derived from opium itself, but also powerful synthetic pain-relieving drugs which have an action like that of the opiates and hence are often referred to as "opiate-like" in their activity.

Of these two groups of drugs, probably the best known are morphine, diamorphine (heroin) physeptone (methadone) and pethidine.

Opium is extracted from the opium poppy – *papaver somniferum* – which is cultivated in India, China, Asia Minor and certain Balkan countries. From powdered opium twenty-five alkaloids are obtained including morphine, codein, thebaine, papaverine and narcotine. In crude form opium has been used in medicine for centuries, but in the last one hundred and seventy years scientific inquiry has gradually isolated the active principles of opium, and has led to the synthesis of opiate-like

Poppy pods used for making opium

drugs. It would be hard to over-estimate the value of the opiates because their powerful pain-relieving effect was for many years all that doctors had to offer their patients for the relief of pain, and in this area their position is still unchallenged. Nevertheless the problems created by their potential for producing dependency have been increasingly recognized and one of the basic tasks of experimental pharmacologists has been to try and develop powerful pain-relieving drugs which do not produce states of dependence. So far this has not been achieved.

Morphine is the most potent of the alkaloids of opium and was isolated in 1803 by a German pharmacist, Seturner. In general morphine is regarded as the point of reference for opiates and opiate-like drugs. Indeed, patterns of dependence are usually referred to as "dependence of the morphine type."

Diamorphine, or, to use its popular name, heroin, is a synthetic morphine-like drug, first made in 1898. Originally it was regarded as a drug likely to help in the treatment of morphine dependence, since at that time it was not expected to produce any dependence. Unhappily, as the world now knows, the truth is exactly the opposite.

Physeptone (methadone) is another synthetic analgesic drug, first produced in Germany during the Second World War. It has considerable uses in medicine, not only for the relief of pain but also for the suppression of cough, and although dependency-producing it appears to give a less severe variety of dependence than that produced by morphine or heroin. In recent years it has been increasingly used in the treatment of morphine-type dependence, as a substitute during withdrawal and, lately, as a more lasting form of replacement treatment (see Chapter 9).

Pethidine is another powerful synthetic analgesic which has found wide use in midwifery because it does not depress respiration to the same extent as does morphine. It, too, has powerful dependency-producing characteristics.

Dependence of morphine type is characterized by a marked tendency for the dependency to develop fairly quickly after repeated injections of small amounts of the drug, whether it be morphine, diamorphine or physeptone. With this repetition of doses is associated the development of tolerance, that is to say the person needs more of the drug to achieve the desired effect. At the same time physical and psychological dependence develops. In fact, with morphine-type drugs physical and psychological dependence are likely to be strong. Oddly enough, the physical ill-effects on the user are not so much produced by the direct effects of the drug, whether in the short or the long term, but are due more to second-order effects from injection with dirty needles and syringes. Thus the regular user of such a drug is likely to suffer from local infections such as abscesses and severe general infections like "blood-poisoning" or septicaemia, or pneumonia. He is also liable to liver-damage from jaundice transmitted through the syringe. In addition, the depression of appetite caused by the drugs brings about loss of weight, and it is common to find users neglecting themselves and the conduct of their lives very considerably, and spending more and more of their time involved with the drug. Self-neglect is very common. Withdrawal from morphine-type drugs produces a characteristic *abstinence syndrome,* that is a group of symptoms which have a physical basis and which are an index of the degree of physical dependence on the drug. These symptoms include yawning, itchiness of the trunk and limbs, salivation, nausea, retching and vomiting, running of the nose, pains in limbs and joints, severe abdominal cramps, diarrhoea, restlessness and general distress.

These symptoms come within hours of the last injection, reach their maximum within twenty-four to thirty-six hours, depending on what drug has been taken, and are gone within four to five days.

(b) The Barbiturates and barbiturate-like sedatives

The barbiturates were first introduced into medicine at the end of the last century. They are all salts of barbituric acid, which is chemically related to urea. Urea is a product of the breakdown of nitrogen containing substances in the body which, when found in excess in the bloodstream, give rise to the condition called uremia. Urea has a depressant effect on the brain and in excess produces drowsiness. Now the barbiturates have been widely used in medicine to promote sleep, in the treatment of epilepsy and also as mild day-time sedatives for anxious people. But they are not without danger and people can become severely dependent on them. There has been increasing recognition of this in recent years, particularly since the 1950s when the characteristics of chronic intoxication with barbiturates were first analysed. However, it is ironic to note that the first case of barbiturate-dependence described in the medical literature was recorded within two years of their appearance.

In recent years there has been an increasing search by pharmacologists for sedative drugs which have similar actions to barbiturates but which are without their dangers. As a result a number of *barbiturate-like sedatives* have been developed. These include such drugs as: glutethimide (doriden), methqualone (melsed), methqualone and diphenyl-hydramine (mandrax). Unhappily, however, though they have been in many respects safer than barbiturates, they are capable of producing a dependency similar to that on barbiturates.

The picture of *barbiturate dependence* is very similar to that found in alcohol-dependence, and for this reason the W.H.O. refers to "dependence of the barbiturate–alcohol type." Thus when reading this section the reader may mentally substitute the term alcohol for the term barbiturate.

In barbiturate dependence, psychological dependence always occurs. Physical dependence usually occurs in cases where the dosage exceeds ordinary medical levels, and when it is taken over a period of weeks; when this happens the physical dependence is severe and very dangerous. Someone who is in a state of physical dependence is, by definition, in a *state of chronic barbiturate intoxication*, and his appearance is just like that of the person intoxicated with alcohol without the smell of alcohol. His walk is unsteady and staggering (ataxia), his speech is slurred (dysarthria) and his mental state is one of muddle and confusion.

The most common variety of barbiturate dependence is probably one of mild psychological dependence in people who have been taking them regularly, often in moderate doses, for years. However, there is a growing number of young people who are subject to physical dependence accompanied by chronic intoxication, and who inject themselves with barbiturates. They choose barbiturates because of their rapid effect when injected, while opiate-takers use them when they are short of opiates.

One of the major hazards of barbiturates is that their level of tolerance does reach a limit, so that no equivalent is found of the extreme degrees of tolerance found in the opiate-taker. For this reason deaths from accidental over-dosage are common.

Nausea, shaky hands, faintness and dizziness are the most common early signs of physical dependence. Withdrawal from physical dependence is dangerous as fits may occur. These can be fatal, for example if vomit is inhaled. Barbiturates also lower people's self-control and may trigger off aggressive and violent behaviour. Where doses are high withdrawal can be complicated by states of confusion and delirium, that is, restless over-activity accompanied by incoherence and hallucinations accompanied by disordered consciousness. Such states can persist for days. Where the drug is injected the complications from a dirty needle will occur together with ulcers at the site of the injection.

2 STIMULANT DRUGS

The largest group of drugs involved here are the amphetamines and amphetamine-like drugs. These have been widely used in medicine since the mid-thirties mainly for their wakening and mild antidepressant action and also to suppress appetite in obesity. Their usefulness has been questioned since mild depression is not adequately relieved by them, nor is appetite adequately suppressed. In recent years there has perhaps been a belated awareness of their ability to produce dependence. There are many varieties available, perhaps the most hazardous being those which contain a small dose of a barbiturate ("blues,' "purple hearts"). They are much more potent when injected. The most widely known is methylamphetamine (methedrine or "speed") which was freely available in this country until 1968, when it was withdrawn from general use on the advice of the Ministry of Health at the time of an epidemic of methylamphetamine self-injection. Amphetamine-takers feel buoyed-up, confident and more cheerful but heavy doses cause irritability, querulousness and eruptions into violence. There is also the risk of developing an *amphetamine psychosis.* This is a mental illness in which the subject's contact with reality is impaired, his thinking becomes disorganized and irrational, and he is beset by ideas of persecution, becomes restless and excited and may hear hallucinatory voices. Such a state of *drug-induced psychosis* may be so severe as to merit treatment in a psychiatric hospital. These conditions were first described by Connell (1955) and are a very real hazard of amphetamine-taking.

Dependence on amphetamine-type drugs is characterized by extreme degrees of psychological dependence. Physical dependence does not occur. The amphetamine-taker is likely to be restless and over-talkative, over-excited and cheerful. This mood gives way suddenly to one of sullen, irritable depression, particularly when the effect of the drug is wearing off during the "come-down."

Tolerance develops quickly so that large doses – greatly in excess of ordinarily prescribed levels – may be consumed by the experienced amphetamine-taker. People taking large doses of drugs such as methylaphetamine (methedrine) often spend a succession of days and nights in a state where they prowl restlessly around doing nothing particularly productive and often repeating a series of acts over and over again. For example, one patient spent whole nights assembling and taking to pieces the mechanisms of clocks and watches; another was constantly "redecorating" his flat.

The other important stimulant drug is cocaine. This is prepared as a crystalline white powder, and in solution is sometimes used in medical and dental practice as a local anaesthetic. When taken

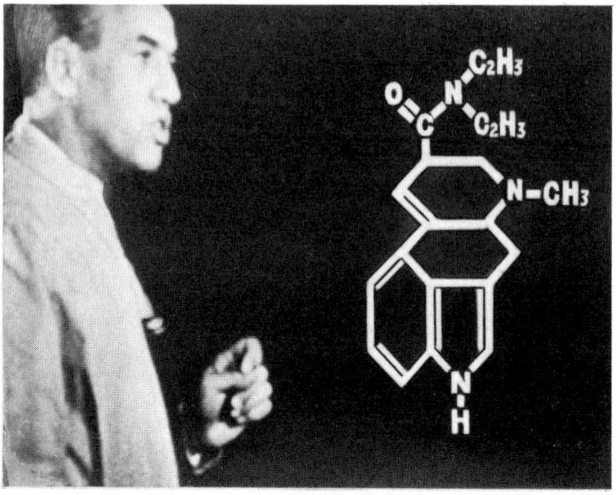

Dr Albert Hofman demonstrates the formula for LSD 25

directly into the bloodstream by injection or indirectly by inhalation it produces an extremely stimulating effect and for this reason has been highly prized by drug-users. Physical dependence does not occur but psychological dependence may be very intense. The hazards of taking cocaine include states of psychotic excitement, itching and strange sensations in the skin, and also cocaine dermatitis (skin disorder).

3 THE HALLUCINOGENIC DRUGS

The hallucinogenic drugs are so named because of their special effect, which is to produce in people quite fundamental alterations in their perceptions of the outside world. Perhaps the best-known drug in this group is lysergic acid diethylamide (or LSD). This drug was synthesized by Hofman in 1938, but he only discovered its hallucinogenic effects in 1943 after unintentionally drinking a beaker of water containing it. LSD is probably the most potent biochemical substance that exists, taken weight for weight.

The important point about many hallucinogenic drugs is that the altered perceptions which they may induce often come to be greatly valued – in many instances over-valued – by the taker, leading him sometimes to alter his whole way of life quite radically. Physical dependence does *not* occur, but psychological dependence, for the reason mentioned already, may be fairly extreme. It is also known that adverse reactions, particularly to LSD, may be quite common. In these adverse reactions the person concerned may feel inexplicably afraid and anxious – often for weeks or months – and he may become very depressed or even be troubled by persistent and distressing feelings of unreality. In addition quite severe derangements of behaviour may occur in which the person loses contact with reality, flees from fancied persecutors, experiences frightening hallucinations – in short develops a *psychotic reaction*. Unfortunately there is no way of predicting who is more prone to such reactions, nor is there any way of predicting when they may occur. Indeed, they have been described as occurring up to eighteen months after taking a hallucinogenic drug such as LSD, although the majority of cases occur within a month or a few days.

The medical uses of hallucinogenic drugs lie in a contentious area. They have been fairly widely used in psychiatric practice but there is little in the way of hard data to establish their role clearly. Their possible usefulness as experimental tools merits further consideration since it is felt by some that their mode of action could throw light on the operation of the brain.

Although the hallucinogenic action of these substances may be the effect that is most sought after, it is probably not widely known that this effect is one of the *least* intense, as has been shown by studies in experimental situations. In fact the most universally found effect is on the autonomic nervous system, that is on those parts of the nervous system that control heart rates, the respiratory rate and movements of the stomach and intestines. The most striking secondary effects are on the subject's *mood*. These effects are apparent long before any hallucinogenic effect occurs, if indeed it occurs at all.

When alterations in perception occur they may or may not be dramatic. What is striking is the *portentous quality* of many of the experiences that people have under the influence of hallucinogenic drugs. Thus the user may have remarkable and intense revelatory experiences which he is incapable of communicating. Any outward sign of benefit that he may claim to have received is very hard to discern and, in the author's view, it is this rather deceptive quality of the hallucinogenic experience which is the most potentially misleading, and can even be malignant.

Cannabis is usually included in the hallucinogenic drugs, but it really merits a section of its own. Synonyms for cannabis include the following: pot, tea, weed, grass, marijuana, hash, hashish, ganja, bhang.

Cannabis. The cannabis sativa plant grows widely throughout the world. The dried flowering tips and shoots of the plant contain a resin with a number of intoxicating substances, the most active principle of which has been isolated and identified as delta l Tetrahydro cannabinol (THC).

Cannabis preparations vary considerably in potency and the percentage of THC present ranges from nearly nil to 2 per cent and varies with the season collected, the climate and the mode of preparation. Cannabis as found in India is prepared in three forms: bhang, the least potent, ganja from cultivated plants, and

Mixing cannabis with tobacco

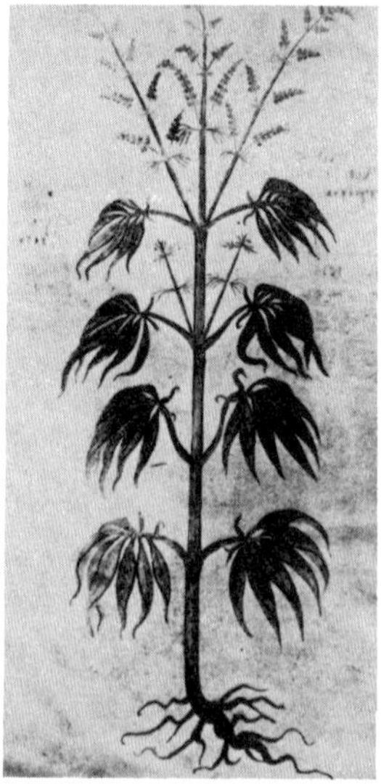

Indian hemp from which cannabis is derived

hashish which is a pure resin from specially grown plants and is said to be the most potent.

The effects of cannabis include feelings of anxiety, mood elevation and distorted perception. Thinking becomes muddled and often the mood is one of breezy insouciance. Hallucinations tend only to occur with potent preparations such as hashish. The physiological effects of cannabis are mainly confined to rises in pulse-rate and blood-pressure.

Physical dependence on cannabis does not occur but there may be quite marked psychological dependence on the substance.

The chief hazards of cannabis usage seem to be perceptual changes which can occur with higher concentrations and also the states of chronic intoxication with cannabis that heavy users can sometimes develop. It appears that in these states the person going around in a state of chronic intoxication with cannabis is unable to think clearly, has poor concentration and is generally unable to cope with the everyday business of living.

In general we can say that cannabis is not a highly dependency-producing drug like heroin or the barbiturates but this does not give it a clean bill of health. Unfortunately it is a substance that seems to invite extremes of opinion, but these will be considered in Chapter 10.

"The Churning of the Milky Way," or the Birth of Hashish

Glue and volatile solvent sniffing. The inhalation of the vapours of volatile solvents obtained in such commonly-available articles as model-aeroplane glue, cleaning-fluid, lighter-fuel, and so on has been widely reported in the United States and to a lesser extent in Japan and Sweden. In the United Kingdom occurrences of this variety of self-intoxication have been relatively infrequent. Here what is striking is that the substances which are valued by the user are relatively easily obtained. The most common source resides in the glue used for making model aeroplanes and also found in plastic cement. The basic organic solvent in these two particular substances is toluene but in fact a wide range of substances have been employed including xylene, benzene, petrol, nail-varnish-remover, carbon tetrachloride (used in home dry-cleaning) and chloroform. Most of these substances, if taken in high enough concentrations, can cause quite severe brain-damage, coma, and even death.

The majority of people involved in what may be called glue-sniffing are relatively young children who either inhale the glue after squeezing it out onto a piece of cloth or else inhale it through a tube or in a plastic bag. After a few deep breaths the youngster feels very exhilarated and cheery, and during a period which may last up to three-quarters of an hour they will show a disturbance of movement and rather slurred speech. The desired effect is first a feeling of exhilaration and secondly a hallucinatory experience which may be highly valued. Thereafter, during the next few hours or even days, the youngster has a hangover period. Groups of glue-sniffers studied in America showed that the regular glue-sniffer is rather a different youngster from the youngster who tries it once only. The "once-only" user is likely to be a perfectly normal child who may have tried it as a result of a dare to "go along" with the others. The regular user on the other hand, tends to be a youngster with quite severe personality problems.

A consideration of this sort of practice is relevant since it demonstrates, yet again, that repeated substance abuse, whatever group the substance may belong to, is likely to be associated with problems relating to the individual himself.

Experimentation may be part of normal experience, whereas continuation of the practice will probably be bound up with the psychology of the individual.

ALCOHOL

Alcohol is a generic term used to describe a class of substances which are in chemical language "hydroxy derivatives of aliphatic hydrocarbons." Alcohol as generally used means ethyl alcohol (C_2H_5OH) – often referred to as ethanol, grain alcohol or proof spirit. Ethyl alcohol is the basic intoxicant in alcoholic beverages whether they are beer, cider, wines or spirits. Alcohol is quickly absorbed from the stomach (about 20 per cent) and from the small intestine (80 per cent). However the presence of food in the stomach delays alcohol absorption. On the other hand carbon dioxide speeds it up, and this is the reason for the rapidly produced states of intoxication that follow the drinking of wines such as champagne. Elimination of alcohol begins soon after absorption, about 10 per cent being excreted unchanged by the lungs and kidneys. The rest is broken down to liberate energy (oxidation). The calories liberated by alcohol are not stored by the body, and since excessive alcohol drinkers tend to neglect their diet this means that though their immediate calorie needs may be met they easily develop nutritional deficiencies which lea to vitamin-deficiency disorders, damage to nerves, etc.

Brain effects

The basic action of alcohol is depressant, in the same way as barbiturates and general anaesthetics are depressant. A summary of alcohol effects correlated with percentage concentration in the blood now follows.

Percentage concentration in the blood	*Effect*
0·05	Lessened restraint, a feeling of disinhibitio Talking more quickly and loudly.
0·10	Speech beginning to be slurred, movemen clumsy. The world seems a brighter place. Companions seem more friendly, prevailin restraints on behaviour are removed. Emotional outbursts may occur. (*NB* This is probably the stage of alcoholic intoxication that most people look for.)

0·20	Drowsy, unable to stand; looking at the ceiling is the preferred position. Standing can only be performed with difficulty. Speech is very slurred. Gait is staggering.
0·30	In stupor. Deaf to the world.
0·40	In coma (like a person in deep general anaesthesia).
0·60 – 0·70	Depression of respiratory and cardiac centres in the brain ----- death.

The general behavioural effects of alcohol are coloured by the person's personality (cheery or quarrelsome), the situation (e.g. wedding or funeral), the amount of drink taken and the company the drinker is with.

Alcohol then is a powerful depressant of brain activity. Its stimulant effects are apparent rather than real and result from a lessening of control by higher centres in the brain.

Physical complications associated with chronic alcoholism include liver-damage. They are usually caused by the poor nutritional state of the alcoholic, vitamin deficiencies and damage to nerves. Ultimately alcohol can cause dementia – that is progressive irreversible brain-damage.

Chapter 3

Some classic examples of drug-taking, ancient and modern

OPIUM IN CHINA

The use of opium is traditionally associated with China, although in fact it did not start there until the seventeenth century. The history of opium-taking in China was recently reviewed by Fields and Tararin (1970) who remind us that the earliest references to opium are found as far back as 4000 BC. Thereafter references to its use as a self-intoxicant and its use in medical practice are found in Egyptian, Greek, and Roman writings. The history of the use of opium in medicine is as old as the history of medicine itself, since it was the first effective substance known to physicians for relieving pain and producing sleep. However, the danger of users becoming dependent on it was certainly recognized by the ancient Romans, who referred to the hazards of chronic opium-taking and the ill-effects suffered by the taker when he was deprived of it. For centuries, however, the use of opium appears to have been confined to the Middle and Near East and hardly to have touched Europe. Opium was probably brought into India in the eighth century by Arab merchants, and in the sixteenth century European travellers described its production and consumption in that country. With the establishment of the Mogul empire in India the production of opium became the virtual monopoly of the Moslem population until the middle of the nineteenth century, long after the British had acquired control of India. Although opium was probably brought into China in the ninth century, its production was mainly confined to India. During succeeding centuries the spread of the opium habit in China became a growing problem, until by the seventeenth century the rulers of China were so sufficiently concerned as to try to exert some control over it. However, since the British were in control of India, the major opium-producing country, it was an enormous source of revenue

The opium-smoker, Inajat Khan, drawn the day before his death in 1616

to the British rulers, who encouraged the growth of opium and the trade with China. Ineffective attempts at suppressing the opium trade were made by the Chinese and culminated in the 1840s with the first of the opium wars between Great Britain and China. There is little doubt that the ultimate object of these wars was to coerce the Chinese into continuing the import of opium into their country. Ultimately British military strength was successful and the opium trade was reimposed on the Chinese. The smoking of opium started after the smoking of tobacco and is said to have been introduced into China from the Dutch East Indies. Whatever the actual sequence of events, there is no doubt that the rulers of China were aware of the fact that vast numbers of people, particularly those of the poorest classes, were rendered inert and apathetic by their excessive use of the drug and spent their slender financial resources on it. International control of the opium trade did not really begin until the early part of the twentieth century, the international agreement of 1912 being a landmark. However, there is little evidence of any decline in opium-taking in China thereafter. When the Japanese invaded the Chinese mainland they deliberately exploited the use of opium as a way of purchasing the

Opium poppy

co-operation and submissiveness of their defeated victims. Thus the spread of opium-taking and -smoking in China may be seen initially in the context of the commercial exploitation of an impoverished people, and subsequently as the exploitation of a vanquished enemy for social reasons. It is said that at the present time opium-use in China has been virtually eliminated as a social problem.

CHATORPAN IN INDIA

There are various examples of what is regarded as addiction but which do not involve substances producing dependency in the true sense of the word. In these cases a society will look upon the addiction as a genuine dependency, constituting a deviant form of behaviour – merely because it lies outside what is commonly accepted as normal. An instructive illuminating example of this sort was described by Vatuk and Vatuk in 1967. The condition is called chatorpan and is found amongst the Hindi-speaking people of Western Uttarpradesh in Northern India. Apparently in this area of India chatorpan is generally regarded by people as a dependent state in which the person involved eats an excessive quantity of sweets (mithai) and spicy snacks (chat) and also by the fact that people who are so involved tend to behave in an antisocial way. It is regarded as antisocial because the person's change in behaviour is supposed to result from his excessive preference for these foods. Men so involved are called "chatora" and women "chatori." There is some disagreement as to whether this behaviour pattern can be regarded as basically a medical problem but there appears to be a consensus of opinion that this excessive eating of sweets causes people to become dependent on them.

However, the authors demonstrate that the phenomenon is illustrative of the ways in which a society views people who behave like this. In the course of their investigations the authors were able to interview doctors, teachers, civil servants and artists, as well as a number of housewives and agricultural workers. They asked them how they regarded the behaviour of people who ate sweet foods to excess. They also investigated the folk sayings and beliefs connected with the phenomenon. It transpired that in Northern India sweet foods play an integral part in social and religious activities. The area is one which produces sugar-cane, so that sweet foods are not rare. In the religious setting sweets are a standard offering at worship and at religious festivals sweets are the normal substances offered in the temples and other places of worship. Sweet offerings also play an important part in marriage rituals and the ceremonies surrounding childbirth and death. Local proverbs, too, contain frequent references to the pleasure experienced in eating sweets.

It appears that it is not so much the fact that the individual eats sweets to excess which is unfavourably regarded, but rather that his over-indulgence evidently coincides with a series of undesirable personality characteristics. The people involved in chatorpan are generally considered by society to be rather worthless, immature people who are likely to be sexually promiscuous. The informants interviewed by the authors described neighbours who were excessive sweet-eaters as having entered into a process of moral and social deterioration. Many of the examples quoted show a remarkable resemblance to the changes in behaviour that are observed in chronic alcoholics and in drug-users. For example, the chronic sweet-eater is unable to afford his needs and will resort to cheating, stealing and other means to obtain more money. Other informants described how chatoras engaged in criminal activity, and were frequently imprisoned. Such individuals are generally regarded as incompetent and inert with little contribution to make to society. Their ultimate fate is said to be one of social degradation where the community regards them as intolerable. It is, of course, very hard to evaluate social attitudes; what is significant are the attitudes themselves. It appears that it is not so much the person's actual dependency on sweets that is the bone of contention; rather it is his excessive self-gratification and it is this that is supposed to lead to personal, moral and social decline.

The investigation by these Indian authors is of importance since, firstly, it is concerned with substances that are relatively harmless, and secondly it demonstrates how a society may come to regard a behaviour pattern not only as abnormal but as anti-social and also deviant.

CANNABIS

Lewin (1931) describes how in 1378 the Emir Soudoun Sheikhouni attempted to prevent the poor people abusing cannabis or Indian hemp by having the plants destroyed and the eaters imprisoned. He also gave orders that people who were convicted in this way should have their teeth removed. Nevertheless, the use of cannabis increased.

This is another example of the way in which societies may place extreme sanctions on the use of various intoxicating substances. Cannabis, however, is of particular interest since it is a substance that has been taken by millions of people all over the world. In general its use is universally regarded as illicit, although traffic in the drug is continually increasing. Perhaps the most recent and most succinct review of cannabis usage is that described by Chopra (1969). He points out first of all that cannabis is surely the substance with the most lengthy history of abuse and makes the point that the habit has spread not only through social use but also through its use in medical and religious settings. It is also a plant that grows wild and is relatively cheap.

Early references to cannabis are found as long ago as 2000 BC when it was referred to as a sacred grass. From the fifteenth to the seventeenth century it was regarded by Indian physicians as being a possible cure for leprosy and a general stimulant. It is likely that cannabis use started in India, whence it spread to Arabia and then to other parts of the world. The ancient Assyrians and

A cannabis-smoker in India today

Greeks knew of its use but, as Chopra has observed, one of its features is the way it has captured the imagination of the credulous and superstitious.

In ancient Hindu medicine it was used as a sedative, to reduce people's appetite and to relieve constipation. In fact it seems to have been used for a very wide range of disorders ranging from asthma to rheumatic pains. This is probably a reflection of the fact that mind-altering drugs may be taken widely in primitive civilizations for a great variety of reasons. Distribution of the cannabis plant is more or less world-wide. A general review of cannabis usage throughout the Middle East, Asia Minor, Central Asia, India and associated countries would suggest that its use is most prevalent amongst poorer members of the population, particularly in Africa, regardless of whether the drug is prohibited or not. It is difficult to quote exact figures in the countries involved since methods of recording data are themselves suspect.

In Europe and America cannabis usage is relatively recent. According to Chopra the smoking of marijuana started in Paris around the middle of the nineteenth century, having been introduced by intellectuals such as Baudelaire and Gautier. It is interesting to note that at that time the intellectuals and artists who used the drug were in the habit of gathering together to enjoy its effects, which they then discussed at great length. On the whole cannabis in Europe has been regarded rather unfavourably by society. It is only relatively recently that the consumption of cannabis amongst young people has increased considerably, particularly in large cities and seaports.

In America the use of cannabis probably started in the early thirties, after being brought in from Mexico. Since then, and particularly since the Second World War, cannabis use has become widespread especially among university students and young people in general. An important social aspect relating to cannabis is the way in which this drug has almost become a badge of adolescent and youthful rebellion today. Confrontation between the liberally-minded young and the older establishment is, of course, commonplace. It involves not only the differing social attitudes to the political and social structure of the country, differing attitudes to basic institutions such as education, law enforcement, and so on; it also involves a polar difference in attitudes towards cannabis. On the whole, older people are likely to regard cannabis as a dangerously seductive substance which may lead to the use of other and more dangerous drugs, whilst youthful attitudes towards cannabis are less cautious, more casual, and much more exploratory. It is from this conflict between the two groups that the demand has risen for some alleviation of the punitive measures that are directed against cannabis takers. Young people are more likely to see it as a supposedly harmless and pleasurable substance and contrast it with the alcohol-drinking of their elders with its known dangers.

If the problem were as simple as this it would resolve itself. Unfortunately it is not so simple. The experience of countries using hemp has been that regular and chronic cannabis usage does lead to states of social inertia and chronic intoxication, loss of appetite and interest, and while there may well be less inherent dangers in the substance *per se* it is likely that it involves social hazards. Further, it is surely undesirable for people of any age to get into states of chronic intoxication through cannabis, alcohol, or any other substance. The occasional cannabis-user may not be running much of a risk, but we cannot say the same about the chronic cannabis-user. It may also be relevant to ask whether society needs yet another intoxicant.

ETHER-DRINKING IN ULSTER

Connell (1965) wrote an elegant and carefully documented account of a nineteenth-century occurrence which illustrates very well the way in which people may move from one intoxicant to another when supplies run short and when a number of local, social and other influences happen to coincide.

The abuse of alcohol has been a well-recognized problem in Ireland and amongst Irish expatriates for many years. During the nineteenth century there was a good deal of illicit distilling. But during the mid-nineteenth century there was also a period of ether-drinking in Ulster. This was surprising since ether is an objectionable drink; it burns the mouth and causes intense nausea and retching. Thus for the alcohol-drinker to turn to ether he must certainly be influenced by powerful forces.

Early in the nineteenth century there had been episodes in Europe and America of intoxication through ether, but these mostly involved people who inhaled ether vapour, thus becoming inebriated rather quickly and feeling generally hilarious. These occasions were often referred to as "ether frolics." They were by no means a general practice and were said to be confined to the upper social classes, including medical men. By the middle of the nineteenth century, although ether was being drunk in small quantities by some members of the professional and upper middle classes it was in no sense a widespread practice – probably because ether tastes so foul. Later in the nineteenth century many fashionable and professional people turned to morphine, and consequently the use of ether began to decline among the well-to-do.

The point emphasized by Connell is that, by contrast, the Ulster epidemic witnessed ether taking a strong hold on a large part of the population in a particular area of this country which was about 1,000 square miles in size and which centred on Cookstown. 50,000 people from a wide range of social classes were said to be regular ether-drinkers and the annual consumption was 17,000 gallons. Most of it was imported from England or Scotland. Villages and market towns often smelt of ether vapour and it was a common sight to see people staggering around under its influence. Ether is a very powerful intoxicant. A small amount absorbed into the bloodstream soon renders a person unconscious. It then is quickly excreted, so that the drinker passes from drunkenness to sobriety and back to drunkenness again in a few hours. Fortunately for the drinker, however, only a small amount is actually absorbed, for it vaporizes very quickly in the stomach causing belching and vomiting. The serious drinker has therefore to work hard at the nauseating task of drinking the stuff.

Perhaps the most interesting conclusions drawn by the author are the reasons for the spread of the habit. First of all ether had been introduced for medical reasons: both for anaesthesia and for various preparations to "calm the nerves." It had also acquired a reputation as a remedy for cholera, following a cholera epidemic in Glasgow.

A number of additional factors seem to have moved the people in this part of Ulster to turn to ether-drinking on a large scale. There had been a vigorous temperance campaign preached by Father Mathew throughout Ireland. Many took the pledge but found they could not manage without some form of self-intoxication. In other cases, ether was prescribed by doctors as a treatment for alcoholics. At the same time the materials for distillation at home became scarce, grain being dear and hard to come by. This problem was aggravated by more vigorous action against illicit distilling. Finally, ether was cheaper than whisky, and virtually under no controls of sale, so that it became an obvious substitute.

The extent of the habit caused widespread alarm: its dangers were written about in medical and lay journals, while anti-ether sermons were preached in churches. Eventually ether was included under the Poisons Act of 1870. Thus the demand gradually declined. The habit was so nauseating that it was more or less self-defeating, and so this strange phenomenon faded away. Curiously enough, although its dangers were widely described there remains little evidence of large numbers of people coming to harm. When grain was cheaper, people took to home-distilling and were again able to enjoy the pleasures of a palatable drink.

PHENACETIN IN SWEDEN

Phenacetin is a pain-relieving, mildly-stimulating drug which has been used in medicine for many years, usually in combination with aspirin, or in a variety of pain-killing tablets which are relatively easy to obtain. Unfortunately, taking phenacetin over a prolonged period and in excessive doses can cause kidney damage leading, in some cases, to kidney failure and death from uraemia.

During the investigation of kidney damage caused by the prolonged taking of phenacetin an interesting story of its abuse was revealed in a small town in Sweden called Husqvarna (Grimlund, 1963). This town's main industry consists of a large factory producing a wide range of goods. At that time it employed 3,000 people. The investigation centred upon the reasons for the very high prevalence of phenacetin-abuse in the town – an abuse which had manifested itself in a high death-rate from uraemia. The trouble started after the First World War during the pandemic of "Spanish" influenza. A local doctor used to prescribe a powder which contained caffein, phenacetin and phenazone. This powder was effective in relieving the severe muscular pains that were a feature of the disease. However, many people who took the powder felt an upsurge of energy through its mildly-stimulating effect. Like the coca-chewers of South America, workers began to assume that the stimulant effects might be useful in the factory and the notion then spread that this would be a way of working more quickly and earning more money. It was not long before the regular taking of the powders spread through the town. The powders could be bought over the counter and soon regular powder-taking became both a local custom and a social habit. Powders would be offered around like cigarettes. Patients in hospital would often receive them as gifts from visitors. It even became customary to present brightly-coloured packets of the stuff to people on their birthdays.

The consequence was that in Husqvarna the death rate from severe kidney-damage was six times as high as that in a larger town nearby. During the investigation of phenacetin and its probable connection with kidney-damage factory-workers were interviewed and given questionnaires – not without difficulty because many were resentful. People were asked why they had started. The commonest reason for starting was given as "pain," and the commonest reported reason for continuing was "to maintain a high output in the factory." It is ironic that people were in no sense dependent on these powders, for when the dangers were pointed out, most people stopped. Here, then, was a classic example of drug-abuse – involving a drug with medical uses which had been taken excessively and for prolonged periods in a manner and for reasons quite inconsistent with ordinary medical practice. It is also a good example of the way in which a drug or a related substance can acquire a reputation in a very short space of time and be taken up by a community as an acceptable practice. In this instance, as we have seen, the results for many were tragic.

STIMULANT-ABUSE IN JAPAN

One of the most remarkable recent examples of widespread drug-abuse occurred in Japan during the period 1945 – 55 (Brill and Hirose, 1969). This was an epidemic of drug-abuse, which in many cases is unique and which can be viewed as a large-scale forerunner of the problem of stimulant-abuse in Sweden and the United Kingdom. Japan is a country that had had relatively few problems of drug-dependence in the past. In this case the stimulant involved was methylamphetamine, a drug which probably has the most dangerous effects of all the amphetamines. The trouble started just after the Second World War. In wartime it had been issued free to troops in order to improve their energy and fighting spirit. After the war it came on to the public market during a period of intense social disorder. At that time, it was not difficult to obtain a wide range of drugs over the counter, and apart from the laws involving the opiates, laws on drug-control in general were not strict. There is little doubt that, in this instance, the rapid spread of methylamphetamine-abuse may be compared to the epidemic spread of an infectious disease.

The first cases were noted in 1945 and were confined mainly to large cities such as Tokyo and Osaka. Cases then spread to smaller towns and rural areas. The most commonly available variety of methylamphetamine was put in ampoules for injection and at first the drug was obtained quite legally. By 1948 some measure of control was achieved by including methylamphetamine in the list of Dangerous Drugs. Later, further laws were passed to discourage the use of "awakening drugs."

Despite these official warnings and controls the habit spread so quickly that by 1954 there were over 2,000,000 people who could be regarded as users and about 500,000 who were regular users. Early cases were found among the upper classes, particularly among members of literary and artistic coteries, but as was to be expected, it spread throughout society as a whole. In poverty-stricken areas it was responsible for a good deal of delinquency and social disasters. The main group involved was that between nineteen and twenty-five, all of whom were male.

This abuse of amphetamines produced its inevitable complications: psychotic states caused by the drug and also the criminality that is associated with drug-seeking.

It has been commented that this situation resembled the spread of an infectious disease: it arose in a population previously unexposed to drugs, and spread with the same speed and virulence as did, say, measles in the islands of the South Pacific – an area where measles had never been found until it was brought there by foreign travellers.

A young "Futen" or hippy in Japan takes up to twenty sleeping-pills at a time to get "high "

At the same time the structure of society in Japan was in some disorder, the people were demoralized by defeat and by the unbelievable chaos that followed atomic attack. Poverty and unemployment were rife. Further, the previously autocratic structure of Japanese society had crumbled and was being replaced by democracy and liberalism imposed by the West.

In due course the epidemic gradually subsided under the influence of legislative measures: amphetamine production was controlled, and indeed, virtually suppressed; compulsory hospital-treatment was given to those found in possession, while manufacturers were given severe penalties.

An important lesson may be learnt from the Japanese experience, namely that social factors are of particular relevance in determining the patterns of spread; if a population is highly vulnerable the drug problem is liable to expand extremely rapidly.

STIMULANT-ABUSE IN SWEDEN

Sweden is a country with an established history of what many would regard as a high level of social stability. Freedom from war and economic distress and the development in the country of a tradition of moderate and progressive social reform has placed it high on the list of those countries where the bulk of the population enjoys not only a high standard of living but also relative freedom from such pressures as unemployment and poverty. It is in many ways the model of a welfare state. It also happens that like other Scandinavian countries Sweden has a long tradition of keeping careful records of the incidence and prevalence of a wide range of illnesses. In addition to this the population is relatively static so that health statistics, etc., from Sweden are likely to be highly accurate and reliable. There was never any evidence of widespread drug-misuse until the decade 1957–67 when the extent of stimulant abuse in Sweden reached such proportions as to constitute a major public health and social problem. The development of this situation has been carefully reviewed by Goldberg (1967).

The relative rarity of drug-abuse in that country was, just as in the United Kingdom, an established fact and there were few references to it in the Swedish literature. In the early thirties small numbers of people who had become dependent on sleeping tablets such as the barbiturates were noted but even in the early 1940s a nationwide survey revealed less than 100 known cases of misuse and these were predominantly people who were takin opiates.

However in the late 1930s the amphetamines became availab in Sweden, when people soon discovered the stimulating and appetite-lowering effect of these drugs. As often happens, the stimulant reputation of amphetamines spread from person to person and it became known that taking amphetamines would alleviate feelings of fatigue and tiredness, would improve a person's ability to work harder, and increase sexual potency. Further there was no doubt that stimulants were quite widely advertised not only in newspapers and other media but also on the radio, where they were recommended as a sort of universal remedy for people who felt tired and lacking in energy. A comn slogan was "two pills are better than a month's vacation." The tablets could be bought without medical prescription until 193 by which time it was apparent that the numbers of amphetamin being consumed was on the increase. When they became availab only on medical prescription there was a reduction in the natio amphetamine consumption, but this was short-lived. During the early 1940s it seems likely that amphetamine-taking was pretty widespread but cases of true misuse were apparently quite rare and cases of chronic dependency on amphetamines seem also to have been rare. Nevertheless by 1943 doctors were advised o the growth of amphetamine consumption and this led to a fall in the sale of amphetamines of approximately 50 per cent. And in 1944 amphetamines were included on the Swedish National Narcotics Drug List. In other words they became subjected to exactly the same restrictions as narcotic drugs. At the same tim it seems quite definite that medical awareness of the dangers of these drugs was echoed by the news media, who began to comment on the possible dangers of the use of amphetamines.

Some idea of the growth of amphetamine-taking may be gathered from the fact that whereas in 1938 400,000 tablets were sold, by 1942 a total of 6,000,000 tablets were sold. As might be expected the largest sales were recorded in the big cities such as Goteborg and Stockholm. And, as ever, the problems of amphetamine-abuse were concentrated in the cities anc were much less common in the country.

Goldberg estimated that in the years 1942–43 there were around 200,000 regular takers of amphetamines in Sweden, that is about 3 per cent of the adult population. Of these 200,000 people probably 140,000 were occasional takers of whom half would take the tablets once in a year and the other half between two and four times in a year. Of the remainder he estimated about 60,000 would have been taking amphetamines between several times in the year at the least and twice in every month, and about 4,000 were probably taking them once a week. He estimated that 3,000 were taking them more or less daily in doses of up to ten tablets a day – the dosage for the other users being in the order of no more than three or four tablets a day. It was reckoned that the number of excessive users was very small, probably around 200, and these were people who would be taking between ten and 100 tablets in one day.

It seems likely that this incidence and prevalence of amphetamine abuse persisted throughout the 1940s. In other words although amphetamine-taking was widespread true abuse was relatively uncommon and represented only about 0·1 per cent of the total number of amphetamine-takers. But from the middle 1950s the picture changed. A small number of people were known to be taking amphetamines and opium in Stockholm but a much more marked change occurred in 1956, probably reaching its peak in 1959.

The change is a clear one, not only as regards the numbers involved but also as to the whole nature of the problem. Previously amphetamine-taking, though widespread, had been almost entirely confined to the taking of pills obtained on a doctor's prescription. However, in the 1950s a different type of amphetamine-taker emerged. These takers were predominantly delinquent youngsters with a history of previous criminal behaviour. They fastened on amphetamines as a highly-valued stimulant drug and began to obtain their drugs almost entirely by illicit means. In addition to this there was a tendency to take amphetamines by self-injection. By this time, of course, the range of amphetamines was fairly extensive, including not only amphetamine and dexamphetamine (dexedrine) but also newer stimulants such as phenmetrazine (preludin) and methylphenidate (ritalin). Once again it is interesting to note that dexamphetamine, phenmetrazine and methylphenidate were all introduced to medical usage on the supposition that these drugs were valuable as stimulants and for suppressing the appetite, but without possessing the dependency-producing qualities of the other amphetamine drugs.

It is clear then that by the middle and late 1950s the problem of stimulant-abuse in Sweden had reached epidemic proportions. A study of the prevalence of drug-usage was carried out throughout the whole of Sweden in 1965 and this indicated that there were at least 1,000 people who were severely dependent on amphetamines at that time. This would correspond to a finding of some 6,500 people in England and Wales. It should be recognized that all the evidence obtainable suggests that the population involved was using amphetamine-type drugs by means of injection. Since that time a number of legal and social measures have been adopte in Sweden with the object of controlling the spread of stimulant abuse. Perhaps the most interesting feature of the whole problem was that stimulant-type drugs became preferable to other drugs. ' use of opiates and narcotic-type drugs accounted for only a very small proportion of drug-users.

It is tempting to speculate as to why amphetamines should hav become the chosen drug in Sweden whereas during roughly the same period the growing drug problem in the United Kingdom involved narcotic drugs, particularly heroin. Clearly there is no simple explanation for this. We have seen that the epidemic of amphetamine-abuse that occurred in Japan following the Second World War must be viewed against the background of a very changed society, not only following defeat in war but in an environment in which basic social changes were taking place. The nation was being transformed into a democratic society, the people were economically deprived and the general morale was at a low ebb. However, in Sweden none of these dramatic and potent social forces were at work. Here was a peaceful, progressive, rather stable nation with a reasonably law-abiding population that had become involved in an epidemic of (stimular drug-abuse extending to a large percentage of the nation's youth and characterized by extensive illegal activity. For instance, although drugs could be obtained on prescription from doctors the drug-users soon learned to divert drugs obtained quite legally into illicit channels. In addition illicit drugs started to be manufactured privately. These practices flourished despite the

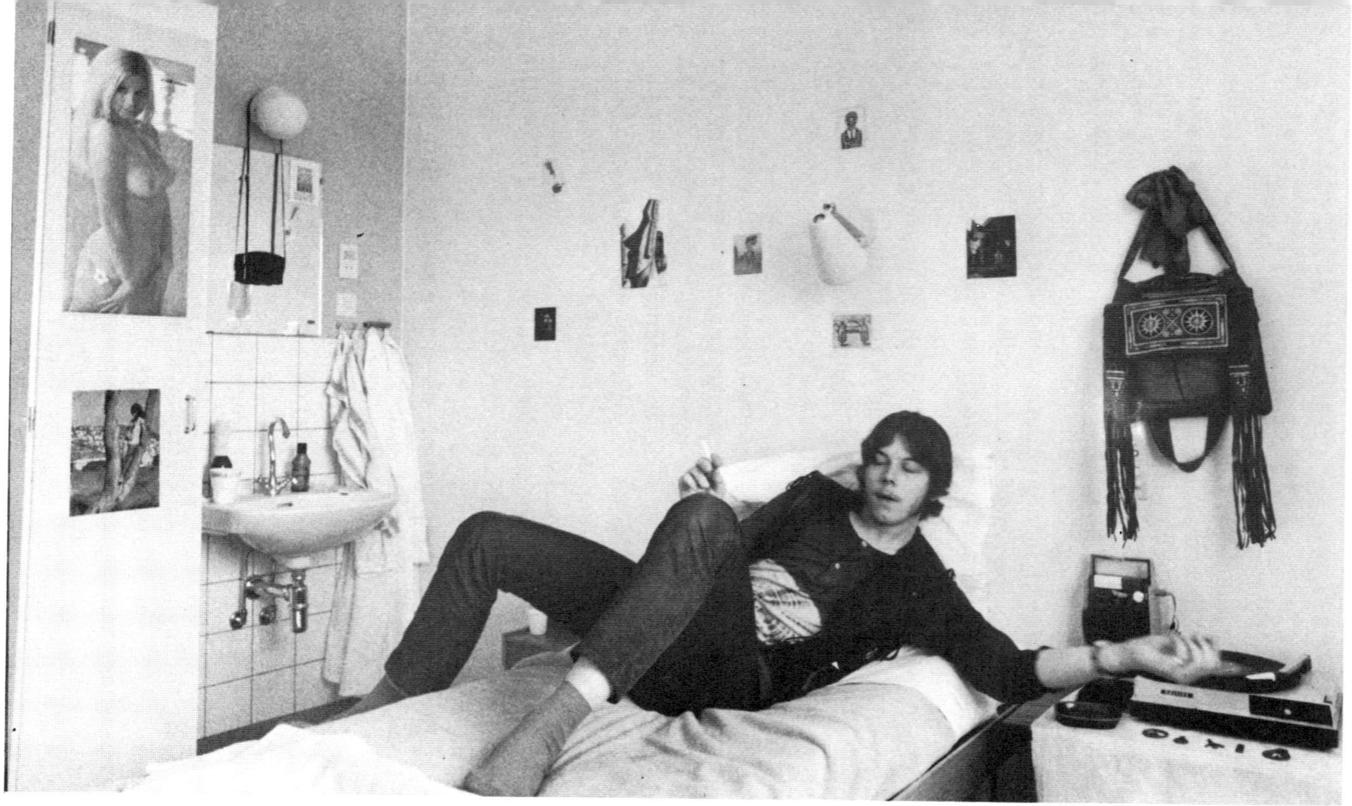

This patient in a Swedish treatment centre is undergoing withdrawal from drugs. His possessions, old symbols of independence, help to preserve his sense of identity

application of vigorous social constraint and a high degree of activity by the police. It is also interesting to note that in both countries, Sweden and Japan, the use of amphetamines started in a perfectly acceptable setting. In Sweden it developed along the lines of traditional medical practice (through prescription) while in Japan it followed on from the use of amphetamines as a means of improving the fighting qualities of the troops and the endurance of the civilian population. In each case the use of these drugs could be regarded as socially acceptable, since at that time the characteristic of producing dependency was presumably not recognized.

Careful studies have been made of the drug-using population in Sweden. Just as in America and in the United Kingdom the bulk of them were found to be young males, many of whom had a background of delinquency, and were using the drug for hedonistic purposes.

In a sense the problem of stimulant-abuse in Sweden remains unresolved, like the problem of drug-abuse in most countries today. It does, however, give us yet another example of how drug-use often starts in a perfectly acceptable way, either through medical prescription, or, as in England in the nineteenth century, through the belief that a particular substance is valuable as a sort of universal remedy. The Swedish example shows us how drug-use may, initially, be relatively widespread in a population, but how the bulk of the people involved may not come to much harm. Then, sooner or later, a dependency-producing drug may acquire an enhanced reputation amongst a section of the population that uses it, or rather abuses it, by taking much higher doses than are suitable for ordinary therapeutic purposes. The hedonistic motives behind this abuse may be related to the individual's background of psychological disorder or they may be related to a general setting of social and economic distress.

In every instance in which drug-misuse reaches epidemic proportions the same pattern of events recurs. The drug is first used by the higher social classes and then spreads throughout the rest of the population. However, a social problem only arises when the drug is taken up and misused by groups of individuals who already have antisocial tendencies. Their behaviour then becomes much more apparent by reason of their drug-habits, and this gives rise to public concern. The public is consequently inclined to put the entire blame on the drug itself, whether it is heroin, amphetamines or alcohol, because the supposed special effects of the drug are the most tangible aspect of the problem. Nevertheless the basic question remains unanswered, namely, what the real significance is of this antisocial behaviour on the part of hedonistic young males.

It may be convenient for society to explain away antisocial behaviour in this context by reference to the drugs alone. However, this will often be a superficial and inadequate explanation. We do know that the actual effects of mind-altering drugs are never as predictable as has sometimes been claimed. Thus every time we are confronted with social problems where drugs are involved we should always investigate the psychology of the individual himself in order to gauge the real significance of his tendencies. Drugs do, of course, frequently trigger off antisocial behaviour in an individual who would otherwise have been socially acceptable. Yet the fundamental question centres upon what it is exactly that society regards as antisocial and intolerable – in contrast to the kind of behaviour it regards as acceptable. The significance of the problem is not related to the number of people involved. Even in the United States, where the use of drugs is far more widespread than elsewhere, it is still far less common than drunkenness. Of course it might be argued that drug-abuse receives special attention because it is found mainly among young people and is associated with a high rate of illness and mortality. However, this is not an adequate explanation since young people engage in other activities which carry higher death rates, such as riding motor-bikes.

It has been suggested that the public concern arises from a *puritanical* preoccupation with this particular pursuit of pleasure and the ill-effects arising therefrom. This may be true, although activities like smoking and over-eating do not attract the same attention, and the link between them and a wide range of physical disorders is obvious. There is probably no complete answer to the question. Nevertheless it should be asked.

THE SPREAD OF DRUG-ABUSE IN THE UNITED KINGDOM

In the early 1960s doctors, psychiatrists, officials of the Dangerous Drugs Department at the Home Office and others concerned with drug problems began to note a disturbing pattern in the increase of dependence on dangerous drugs such as heroin. The background to the growth of these problems has been reviewed by a number of authors (Bewley, 1966; James, 1967; Willis, 196 Spear, 1969; Glatt *et al.*, 1968).

For years England has been regarded by countries such as the United States which had expanding problems of drug-dependence as being particularly fortunate in that their drug problem was relatively small. Though morphinism had been prevalent in the latter part of the nineteenth century, as also had the sporadic misuse of stimulant drugs such as cocaine, on the whole the casual use of narcotic drugs had been fairly limited and there was little evidence of widespread use by youthful people. Over the years the Home Office had kept careful watch over the number of people involved by the simple means of inspecting pharmacists' records of dangerous drugs prescribed for patients. When a name began to appear frequently in a particular pharmacists' list it was easy to check on what was happening and to identify the pattern of drug-dependence.

Up to the Second World War the majority of dangerous-drug-addicts were people receiving prescriptions for morphine. There had been a rise in the use of morphine and cocaine after the First World War, when cocaine was added to the regulations appertaining to dangerous drugs. This happened because soldiers on leave from the Western front had been obtaining cocaine in London and taking it as a stimulant. After the First World War a number of notable examples of morphine- and cocaine-use appeared in the national Press from time to time, but on the whole the problem was kept under control. In 1926 the Rolleston Committee looked into the accepted medical practice of prescribing dependency-producing drugs for known addicts. They reached the general conclusion that prescription was a humane medical practice that was suitable to those addicts who had a clear history of repeated treatment failures, and who could not be weaned from a particular drug but could be "maintained" on it. It is probable that many of the drug-users during the inter-war period may have developed their habit in the late twenties, and were more likely than not to have been solitary neurotic drug-takers. In addition there was a high percentage of people who had developed their dependence during the course of medical treatme that is to say "therapeutic addicts." Further, a small coterie were known to be involved with morphine and heroin in a non-therapeutic setting. The numbers were so small as hardly to present a social problem that was in any way serious. Cannabis-usage was relatively infrequent and confined mainly to merchant-seamen in seaports. During the war cannabis offences showed a rise but again these mainly involved merchant-seamen.

With hindsight it can now be shown that the first sign of change in drug-usage in this country occurred shortly after the 1939–45 war when there was a rise in cannabis offences. These involved members of the West-Indian immigrant population and various professional jazz musicians. But there was no immediate rise in the numbers of people taking morphine and there remained, as ever, a small quota of dangerous-drug-addicts who were physicians, nurses, and others with access to drugs.

By 1950 it was clear that cannabis-usage was on the increase. An important case of drug-trafficking occurred in 1951 (Spear, 1969) following a break-in at a hospital pharmacy. Large quantities of heroin, cocaine and morphine were stolen and subsequently it was discovered that these drugs were being sold illicitly in the West End of London. Some months later the man concerned was arrested and was found to have been formerly employed in the hospital concerned. His arrest and the identification of his customers revealed fourteen people who were taking heroin, cocaine and morphine and who had previously been unknown to official agencies. His subsequent imprisonment lead to the identification of a total of sixty-three people who could be connected with him directly or indirectly.

By 1960 the trend was alarming, for in this year the Home Office first got to know of someone under twenty who was addicted to heroin. During the years that followed although the numbers of morphine-takers remained fairly steady the increase of young heroin-addicts showed a steady growth rate, as will be seen from Graph I.

There is little evidence to suggest that the average "pre-war" drug user tended to congregate in subcultures, but by the 1960s this position was entirely reversed. Certainly there had been a small group of artists and intellectuals just before the war who were known to be heroin-users, but there is little evidence to suggest that they spread the habit. By the 1960s London in

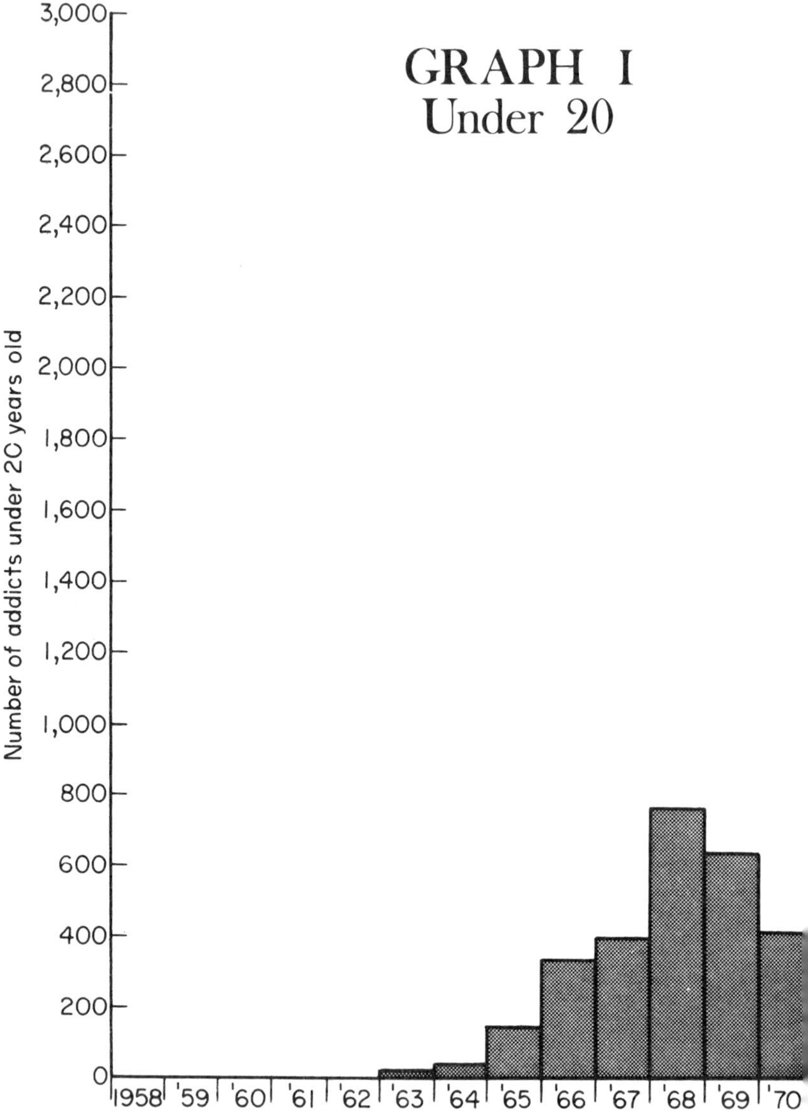
GRAPH I
Under 20
Number of addicts under 20 years old
3,000
2,800
2,600
2,400
2,200
2,000
1,800
1,600
1,400
1,200
1,000
800
600
400
200
0
1958
'59
'60
'61
'62
'63
'64
'65
'66
'67
'68
'69
'70

particular, saw the beginnings of subcultures formed by young drug-users. Many of these youngsters had drifted away from home and lived in parts of London where transient dwellers were commonplace. They tended to congregate, too, in the Soho area which had long been a refuge for young drifters.

Heroin could be obtained on a doctor's prescription comparatively easily. Doctors who took on such youngsters often found their surgeries swamped by large numbers claiming to be addicts. A great deal has been said and written about the "over-prescription" of heroin at this time and undoubtedly there were examples of venal doctors. However, despite the activities of the venal and gullible there were a number of doctors who did their best to cope with a growing number of very demanding patients. Such doctors were working in isolation in general practice, unsupported by the ancillary services of a hospital, so that the basic service that they could offer to the patient was nothing more than the prescription of the drug that they craved. In many instances they found it very hard to believe that the patients might be deceiving them. What happened in very many cases was that patients received drugs in excess of their needs and sold the surplus. In defence of doctors who have been vilified for over-prescription it should be said that frequently their motives were well intentioned, that they certainly achieved no financial gain and that indeed their personal lives were continuously disrupted by importunate patients.

Hospital beds for the treatment of drug-users were hard to come by and various predictions were made about the likely outcome of the general trend. The report of the Interdepartmental Committee then recommended the setting up of treatment centres in the hospital service where the heroin-addict could have heroin prescribed for him on a "maintenance" basis by licensed doctors. The object was to achieve some sort of rational control of the situation and at the same time to discourage the production of an illicit market in such drugs. The report recommended that such centres be supported by facilities for research and treatment and ultimately by rehabilitation measures.

At this period and even while heroin was daily being proclaimed in the various media as the most difficult problem of all, there was an expansion in the taking of stimulant-tablets such as the various amphetamine drugs and also self-injection with stimulant such as methylamphetamine. A number of doctors had prescribe methylamphetamine taken by self-injection as a substitute for cocaine. However, it soon became clear that injectable methylamphetamine was a major source of psychiatric danger because of the hazards of psychosis and also because of the fact that people continuously intoxicated with methylamphetamine went around in an excited, often irritable and aggressive manner, or became very depressed when the drug was unobtainable. They thus presented a growing social menace. Since the amphetamines do not produce any physical dependency it hardly seemed justifiable to continue prescribing them, and it was agreed with the Ministry of Health that the prescription of methylamphetamine be discontinued. This proved to be a successful manoeuvre; although patients were very unhappy at the time the majority survived well enough. However, it is likely that some changed from methylamphetamine to either heroin or methadone.

The growth of the whole problem has, of course, to be viewed clearly in the context of expanding drug-use involving drugs of all sorts. Since 1968, at least self-injection with crushed sleeping-tablets and the contents of sleeping-capsules of the barbiturate and non-barbiturate type became another problem of drug-dependence. In general the population involved today are predominantly young. It is also becoming apparent that here, as in America, a younger generation is becoming more "drug-oriented."

As we have seen, the picture in the United Kingdom right up until after the Second World War, was one of a few hundred known narcotic drug-users most of whom were dependent on morphine. Their dependency was therapeutic in origin. There was also a hard core of doctors, nurses, and people who were exposed to drugs in their professional capacity, but the number of non-therapeutic drug-users was small.

Since the increase in the problem subsequent to the late 1950s there have been many reports describing demographic details of drug-users studied in hospital and in prison. These include those of Bewley (1969), Hewetson and Ollendorf (1964) and Gillespie *et al.* (1967).

It is perhaps striking that a study carried out by Schur (1962) in England tended to confirm early speculations about the nature

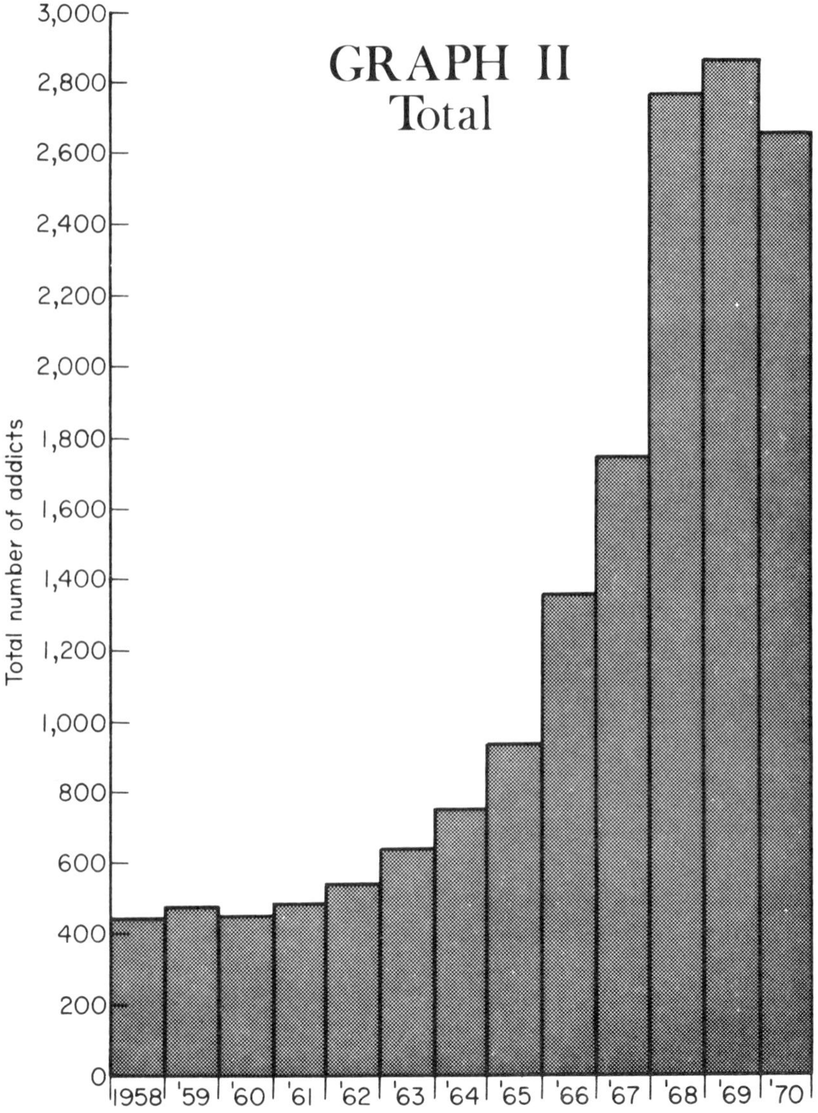
GRAPH II
Total
Total number of addicts
3,000
2,800
2,600
2,400
2,200
2,000
1,800
1,600
1,400
1,200
1,000
800
600
400
200
0
1958
'59
'60
'61
'62
'63
'64
'65
'66
'67
'68
'69
'70

of the English drug-using population. The author looked at occupation, social class, age, sex, marriage, sex-life, onset of drug-habit, occupational adjustment, delinquency and so on, and commented on the high representation of people in the medical and allied professions. He also pointed out that a high proportion of the addicts studied came from social classes 1 and 2, and that addicts tended to be aged over thirty.

Unfortunately the study was carried out at a time when the drug-using picture in England was changing. It failed to demonstrate this change adequately, although with hindsight it is clear that the changing elements were present at that time. As far as Britain is concerned, Schur's findings are no longer at all representative at the present time. The reports of Hewetson and Ollendorf (1967), Gillespie *et al.* (1967), Bewley (1969), Willis (1969), James (1969) suggest a wider spread of drug-usage throughout the social classes and also bring out the links between drug-usage and delinquency.

The number of drug-users known to the Home Office between the years 1958–69 is recorded in Graph II.

As for the distribution of drug-dependency between the sexes, the ratio appears to be five men to one woman. A definite fall in the age of onset is evident: the first recorded addict under twenty years of age was registered in 1960; thereafter the numbers increased many hundredfold. The findings of Bewley (1969) and Willis (1969) reiterate the fact that in general the occupations enjoyed by drug-users have a lower social status than that of their parents. These findings also show that the majority of subjects are unmarried. The figures described by Willis (1969) indicate a history of parental loss through separation or divorce. It also appears that among the parents of drug-users there is a higher incidence of psychiatric disorders, alcoholism and delinquency than in the parents of control subjects. Indeed, the pattern bears a close resemblance to psychiatric patients in hospitals who are not drug-users.

Chapter 4

Studying the problem

Early descriptions of the effects of drugs and alcohol relied upon a variety of writings, and in particular accounts given by explorers in foreign countries of particular methods of self-intoxication. At a later stage we find accounts of drug- and alcohol-abuse written by doctors, clergymen and reforming laymen who realized that these substances were giving rise to social and medical problems. Such accounts are useful but limited ways of collecting information; they would be regarded as rather naive at the present time and of little use in any serious attempt to evaluate the extent of a problem in a particular country. Western countries are increasingly attempting to collect data about the numbers of drug- and alcohol-users, but it should be realized that this is a difficult task. Two terms in particular that need to be clarified are *incidence* and *prevalence.*

Incidence of a condition in a given community – whether it be of tuberculosis, syphilis, alcoholism, drug-dependence, or any other infectious disease – refers to the number of new cases that are notified to the authority collecting information. Prevalence refers to the number of cases that are found to be present at a definite point in time. It is sometimes called *point prevalence.* The data regarding both the incidence and prevalence of conditions such as alcoholism and drug-dependence are usually gleaned from such sources as hospitals where patients have been admitted for treatment, from records of the numbers of convictions for offences involving either alcohol or drugs and also from figures relating to the number of arrests made by the police for such offences. The last of these methods may, however, be misleading. A good example of how wrong impressions can be gained is provided by the contrast found in two major cities in the United States of America, namely New York and Los Angeles. New York city has a population of around eight million and the annual arrest-rate for drunkenness is about thirty thousand.

Los Angeles, which has a population of two and a half million, has an annual arrest-rate of about one hundred thousand. The disproportionate percentage differences between the two cities is accounted for merely by the fact that in recent years a judicial decision in New York determined that arrests for drunkenness should only be made where the person concerned had been involved in some form of disorderly conduct. In the same way hospital records can be misleading. They may, for instance, refer only to people who have been admitted to hospital for mental illness associated with the use of alcohol. This would apply to the figures available for the nineteenth century and the early part of the present century, but of course figures of this kind do not represent the real extent of the problem in any community.

Techniques of investigation are increasingly being employed today whereby the investigators become involved with a community and make direct contact with a wide range of social agen involved with patients. These investigators interview a representative section of the inhabitants of a particular locality; they visit families in their homes and try to determine the approximate incidence and prevalence of a particular condition.

Recognizing that somebody is an alcoholic or is dependent on drugs involves applying what is basically a medical diagnosis, although this does not make it the province of a medically-qualified person. If this were the case many such people would often lack attention altogether, since doctors have in the past tended to opt out of the treatment of drug- and alcohol-users.

Before someone can be categorized as drug-dependent or as an alcoholic both a medical and a social diagnosis is required. We rightly tend to regard the medical role as important in these cases because the medical and psychiatric issues involved are fundamental. None the less the methods of assessment used are similar to methods of social, medical, and psychological inquiry that are applied in many other areas. These include obtaining a history from the person himself and from as many other informants as possible, so that a detailed picture can be built up of his family and personal background, his early development, schooling, occupational history, exposure to delinquent behaviour and so on. It is also necessary to know about the previous history of physical or psychiatric illnesses and complications. The object is to try to clarify as precisely as possible the extent of the problem in each individual case.

The psychological assessment of people attempts to make as accurate and objective an assessment as possible of their intellectual abilities and personality characteristics and is found to be of considerable value in trying to understand the possible causes of an individual's involvement in substance abuse.

BIAS

Early psychiatric writings about alcohol and drugs contain a strongly moralistic flavour. Here it is worth noting that moralizing has not disappeared in the twentieth century; it tends to go on in a more covert form. "Observer bias," that is to say the influence of the observer's emotional involvement, is a well-recognized phenomenon and can result in terms like *alcoholic*, *drug-addict* and *psychopath* being used rather loosely – sometimes almost as epithets.

Class bias, too, is important and perhaps far more relevant than may be realized. It was shown, for instance, in a study in the United States (Holinshed and Redlich) that in a particular area the social class of the individual under investigation not only determined the psychiatric diagnosis that was made but also the sort of treatment he was likely to receive. This class bias has not yet been shown to have occurred in the United Kingdom, but its appearance in the United States is significant and demonstrates how "objectivity" can be subtly undermined. It is important to realize that quasi-scientific and semi-objective pronouncements may be made by an observer about the people he is investigating and that these may be little more than the expression of value judgements arising from the attitudes of the observer's own social class. For example certain modes of behaviour may be judged to be "antisocial" because middle-class people have so defined it. To a large extent behaviour comes to be regarded as either normal or abnormal as a result of middle-class attitudes, and a great many value judgements and pronouncements concerning the behaviour of people with a lower social status are made by those possessing superior social status. The words *addict*, *alcoholic*, *criminal*, *delinquent*, or *psychopath* should call into question the significance of these terms or labels, and the

A relief from boredom. Young people living in deprived circumstances often turn to "speed" for kicks

qualifications of those who have applied them. Properly used they may be valuable tools in the study of human behaviour. Improperly used they reduce the level of the discussion to that of a parlour game. Moreover, if these labels have been incorrectly applied they may stick to the victim throughout his whole life, and to his great personal disadvantage. This in itself can constitute a great handicap. The need to feel superior, in all sorts of ways, is strong in all of us but it has to be resisted if we are to avoid categorizing individuals on the basis of the projection of our own guilt, nourished by social bias.

The diagnosis of a physical disorder is a refined and precise technique today, and in the behavioural sciences it is also a valuable exercise. However, where one is making a social diagnosis the matter is not so easy. There will often be differences in countries in the way in which the question of drug-dependency is viewed by members of the community, purely because of the public image of the drug-user or the alcoholic. For instance, in America, where the question of drug-dependence has been greatly influenced by the enforcement of law, the prevailing public image of the drug-user has been of someone who is basically antisocial and delinquent, and only with great difficulty has it been possible to modify that image slightly in recent years. In the United Kingdom drug-dependence has tended to be regarded more as an illness, so that in general the public image of the person who is dependent on drugs is more likely to be that of someone who is sick rather than criminal.

A FIELD STUDY

The difficulties of accurately estimating the numbers of drug-users in a population have already been touched upon. Its importance became crucial when the increase of drug-use amongst young people began to attract public concern. The problem of numbers was frequently the subject of comment, much of it informed but some of it rather sensational. References in the daily Press were made to the possibility that figures produced by the Home Office Drugs Department might well represent "the tip of the iceberg." A number of rather bold assertions were made, often on the basis of interviews with a handful of young drug-users. Many of these drug-users may well have been

A heroin-addict injecting himself in London's Soho

exhibitionists, and only too ready to paint a highly-coloured picture of the situation.

By 1969 there had been a number of reports published (Glatt, 1967; James, 1967; Bewley, 1966; Willis, 1969), all of which were based on drug-users studied in hospital or in prison. A good example of an alternative method of study was provided by Kosviner *et al.* (1968).

The method used in this latter case involved a team of research-workers investigating the extent of heroin-use in a relatively compact area. The object was not so much to count heads but rather to try to draw a picture of the subculture of drug-users and also tentatively to look into possible social influences contributing to their habit of drug-use.

The town studied was small with a population of under 100,000. It had a university and, as the authors commented, "an unusually high proportion of middle-class people." Members of the university were excluded from the study unless they happened to be local residents. The term "heroin-user" was employed to refer to people who had been taking heroin regularly during any of the preceding three months of the investigation's duration. At first contact was made with four users who attended a group directed by a local psychiatrist. Other drug-users were then introduced through these initial four. At the same time the researchers rented an office and an apartment in the centre of the town and it became an informal meeting-place for people with drug problems where they could feel free, in a non-institutional setting to talk about anything whatsoever to a research team that was very much of their own age-group. There was no occasion for fear or constraint.

The team collected the names of forty-seven people suspected to be heroin-users. Thirty-one of them were found to be authentic users, ten were not, and six had gone elsewhere. They also managed to find six heroin-users who were not known to any official agency. The investigators made careful case-histories of those involved with drugs and also collected information about the social and family backgrounds of the subjects, their education and occupational histories, their health records and delinquent behaviour. It was possible to verify the subjects' accounts from official records, hospitals, social-workers and other sources.

One of the team's more striking findings was that they were unable to demonstrate a single common characteristic shared by all the users they interviewed. This tended to confirm their previous suspicion that the "typical" addict does not exist. They commented that perhaps the most common characteristics of the group were that in general they came from backgrounds with a relatively high social status and also that they tended to show a pattern of academic failure despite having had good opportunities. It was suggested that middle-class youngsters influenced by academic pressure and high family expectations might possibly turn to heroin as a means of escaping from stress. It was also suggested that, for some youngsters, taking heroin was something positive – an act of rebellious defiance. Further speculation was offered as to whether drug-taking was a more attractive form of illicit gratification for some than for others. On the other hand there was no evidence that the group resembled in any way the aimless, purposeless drifting youngsters –

basically delinquent – that had been described by Chein *et al.* (1964) in a study in New York.

Perhaps one of the most valuable aspects of the study was that it was timely, thorough and essentially a prospective one in which the collection of data was, and is, an ongoing process; people initially contacted could be, and were, followed up. Reports were made one year later. A number of lessons were learned. A containment unit was set up in the town to control the quantities of heroin prescribed by licensed doctors. This unit became the only licit source of heroin supply. From early 1968 it was concerned primarily with heroin-takers, so that although the total number of daily heroin-takers did not rise in the year it proved impossible to make any accurate comment about changes in the misuse of other drugs in the area. No doubt many changes did occur, for patterns of change in drug-use are normal in most areas. Overall, they reported on fourteen newly-discovered heroin-users in the year – including not only chronic addicts but occasional heroin-takers.

This type of investigation is of value because it contributes positively to the understanding of what we may call the "natural history of drug-dependence." Hitherto there has perhaps been undue emphasis on taking cross-sections of drug-users, describing the characteristics found, drawing conclusions and more or less leaving the matter at that.

Basic information of course *is* needed since it contributes to the central body of knowledge, but in the long-term study of a chronic disorder it is time that counts. It is easy to speculate on data obtained by the cross-sectional method; this is rather like looking at a school photograph and predicting what is going to happen to the group. However, knowledge about a complex social problem is gleaned over a period of time, and it is a laborious process. Unfortunately because of the emotionally-charged atmosphere that surrounds drugs there is a background clamour for as much instant information as possible, in the hope that this will illuminate a dark area and give the answer to the problem. Prospective research is time-consuming, often wearisome and tends to lack the superficial attractiveness of hastily amassed data. Nevertheless in the long term it is more rewarding.

Chapter 5

Alcoholism: history and definitions

A HISTORICAL NOTE

The medical and social study of alcohol-abuse has developed in fairly recent times. Towards the end of the eighteenth century the social and physical effects of heavy spirit-drinking in England became a matter of public concern because the large numbers of people involved presented an appalling public spectacle. Spirits were so cheap and plentiful that it was quite common to see people lying "dead drunk," or nearly so, in the streets. Social reformers, the clergy and medical men began to interest themselves in the problem. The passage of effective laws controlling the sale and distribution of alcohol had some effect in starting to control public drunkenness. Further, the improvement in social and economic conditions, increased employment and all-round social betterment removed large areas of grotesque squalor and many people no longer attempted to soften the hopelessness of their lives with alcohol. But this did not abolish alcohol-abuse – only its cruder manifestations. During the past hundred years or so, and particularly during the past fifty years, the study of alcohol-abuse has developed along more scientific lines – involving medical, social and psychological inquiry into its causes and effects.

THE TEMPERANCE MOVEMENT

The problems created by drugs such as opiates and cannabis were increased when the practice of smoking tobacco made it possible for people to absorb larger amounts of intoxicants into the blood from the lungs. In the same way many of the damaging consequences of alcohol-abuse followed the discovery of the distillation of alcoholic spirits. Ancient references to drunkenness caused by beverages such as wine are frequent, but the real trouble started when spirits were first invented.

Cruickshank's "The Drunkard Children." (The artist was a member of Temperance League)

This has been particularly true in Northern Europe, where the cold and rainy climate makes spirit-drinking especially attractive.

In England spirits were cheap and easily obtained until the early part of the eighteenth century, when liquor laws were passed which achieved some control over alcohol consumption. But although laws were mainly concerned with an attempt to check a social nuisance and disorder, the effect was little more than to cause a gradual decline in spirit-drinking. The London spirit-shops put up signs saying "Drunk for one penny – dead drunk for two pence – straw for nothing," and in 1743 Lord Lonsdale was able to say in the House of Lords "In every part of this great metropolis whoever shall pass along the streets will find wretchedness stretched along the pavement, insensible and motionless and only removed by the charity of passengers from the danger of being crushed by carriages or trampled by horses or strangled with filth in the common sewers – these liquors not only infatuate the mind but poison the body, they not only fill our streets with madness and our prisons with criminals but our hospitals with cripples. Those women who riot in this poisonous debauchery are quickly disabled from bearing children, or produce children diseased from their birth." The statement was inaccurate in certain respects, but it was to the point.

It was this sort of public statement that probably gave birth to the Temperance Movement. People began to be sickened by the public effects of drink and looked for ways of reducing the misery caused by excessive spirit-drinking. At first, as might be expected, the matter was one of socially-expedient reform, but soon medical men became interested. In 1804 Dr Trotter of Edinburgh (the Scots as usual were ahead of their time in social reform) published a book on the effects of alcohol and in the same year Dr Benjamin Rush of Philadelphia published a similar work. Within the next few years the organization of a Temperance (Moderation) Movement started in the USA.

The first Temperance Society in the USA started in Saratoga, New York, and in 1813 a Society for the Suppression of Intemperance was founded in Massachusetts. The movement made great progress under the influence of the churches. By 1833 there were 6,000 local societies in many American states with more than 1,000,000 members. The earliest European organization started in Ireland – it is said in the small town of

Skibereen in 1818. (Skibereen was always a remarkable place; the newspaper *The Skibereen Eagle* once warned the Emperor of Austria that it had its eye upon him.)

In 1829 the earliest really effective organization came into being, namely the Ulster Temperance Society. In 1831 the British and Foreign Temperance Society was started in London and Queen Victoria became its Patron on her accession.

Unfortunately the Temperance Movement suffered many serious setbacks not so much at the hands of brewers and distillers, but because people in the movement began to differ over what precisely Temperance meant. Initially it meant abstaining from spirits and being moderate, but later the more vigorous members of the Societies voted for total abstention as the only acceptable goal. This was later nicknamed "teetotalism."

The most remarkable temperance-worker in history was Father Theobald Mathew of Cork. During the late 1830s to the mid 1840s he travelled all over Ireland preaching temperance with vigour and enthusiasm. Thousands flocked to hear him and took the pledge in large numbers. In 1841 it was reckoned that the number of abstainers in Ireland was over four million and in three years the consumption of spirits in Ireland fell from over 10,000,000 gallons to just over 3,000,000. It has to be conceded that this success cannot be entirely laid at the feet of Father Mathew, for this was a period of intense poverty, famine and emigration.

By the latter part of the nineteenth century the Temperance Movements began to lose a great deal of their influence. The inescapable fact is that alcohol is a commonly-accepted social beverage. A recent estimate in the United States suggested that 70 per cent of the population drink alcohol, at least on social occasions and usually more frequently. The emphasis nowadays is not so much on abstention from alcohol as on the early recognition of its dangers. A recent suggestion has been to recognize that people *will* drink and that perhaps the best course would be to educate children early as to the dangers of uncontrolled drinking. Equating alcohol with virility, teaching people to "hold their liquor," student bout-drinking – these are practices to be discouraged and replaced by attempts at teaching people to compromise with a dangerous intoxicant. In the United Kingdom, though the Temperance Movement may have lost the vigour

Portrait of Father Mathew

of its nineteenth-century image, the main survivor of those stormy Victorian days is the United Kingdom Alliance which still urges temperance and demonstrates in its publications the value of moderation. It has also urged public attention to the connection between alcohol and road accidents and deaths.

At present Western society is witnessing a fair degree of public tolerance towards the use of alcohol as a socially-acceptable beverage. A state of uneasy compromise has been reached whereby private drinking is tolerated and encouraged but public intoxication is regarded unfavourably. Acute alcoholic intoxication or simple drunkenness is, within limits, tolerated by society provided the user does not break the law or make a public spectacle of himself. At festive and semi-ritual occasions, for example farewell parties, weddings, reunions and so on, drunkenness becomes part of socially acceptable behaviour. It is assumed that people are able somehow to develop their own system of handling alcohol; a man who "holds his liquor" is favourably regarded. At the same time it *is* recognized that if someone's drinking habits interfere with his personal life or his work this represents an undesirable situation which is morally unacceptable. Thus the condition of chronic alcoholism has come to be regarded more and more as a disease affecting the individual rather than a straightforward social menace.

The WHO defines alcoholics as "those excessive drinkers whose dependence on alcohol has attained such a degree that it shows a noticeable mental disturbance or an interference with their bodily and mental health, their interpersonal relations and their smooth social and economic functioning; or who show the prodromal (that is, warning) signs of such development." This is a comprehensive definition of chronic alcohol-abuse which touches upon all the areas which are affected by chronic excessive drinking in the long term.

E. M. Jellinek, who died in 1963, is generally acknowledged to have been the leading expert in the study of alcohol-abuse in this century. In his now classic work *The disease concept of alcoholism* (1960) he stated quite definitively the proposition that alcoholism is best comprehended as a *disease process* and a disease process in which physical damage becomes more progressive with the passage of time and with the consumption of increasing quantities of alcohol. He went further and made the

Archbishop Manning administering the pledge on Clerkenwell Green, 1872

important observation that the causation of chronic alcoholism could be recognized in various syndromes of alcohol-use. The word *syndrome* is a term usually applied to recognizable signs and symptoms of a disease process which point towards not only diagnosis but also causation and outcome.

Jellinek proposed that alcoholics be divided into five groups: alpha, beta, gamma, delta and epsilon.

Alpha alcoholism was regarded by Jellinek as dependence on alcohol at a psychological level only, in which the person uses alcohol as a barrier between himself and his problems. Alpha alcoholics are said to suffer from a non-progressive variety of the disorder in which nevertheless the subject can control the amount of liquor he consumes.

Beta alcoholism is recognized by the appearance of the physical complications of alcoholism such as liver damage and damage to the brain and nervous system. In Beta alcoholism physical or psychological dependence may occur.

Gamma alcoholism is characterized by the fact that the drinker develops a tolerance to alcohol, that is to say his body can more readily cope with increasing quantities and this involves him in drinking more and more to meet his needs. Jellinek suggested that in these cases there occurs some basic change in bodily metabolism at a cellular level which underlies the increased tolerance. The gamma alcoholic, who suffers from an intense degree of physical dependence, is likely to develop physical withdrawal symptoms when he is deprived of alcohol. He is a "true alcohol-addict," and the physical dependence is associated with craving for drink. This variety of alcoholism must be regarded as potentially the most harmful since it appears to be the most progressive type. Ultimately it leads to the most serious damage to personal and public health.

Delta alcoholism is characterized by a persistently raised blood-alcohol level, inability to abstain for long periods and some control at intervals between.

Epsilon alcoholism is similar to what used to be called "dipsomania," that is excessive alcohol abuse from time to time.

Certainly the patterns described by Jellinek coincide with those that have been observed by many workers in the field. Others maintain that chronic alcoholism is not so much a series of categories of a disorder; rather, they view alcoholism as a continuum along which the various types described by Jellinek are seen to exist, and these types are regarded as special highly-recognizable examples of the process. Many hold that chronic alcoholism or "problem drinking" has to do primarily with loss of control over alcohol intake. This may then develop in accordance with a number of different patterns of abuse which are, in effect, sequels to loss of control over drinking.

RECOGNIZING THE PATTERNS OF ALCOHOLISM

In chapter 2 it was pointed out that the type of dependence produced by barbiturates and barbiturate-like drugs is exactly similar to that produced by alcohol, in both its physical and its psychological manifestations. In both conditions, severe fits and states of confusion and delirium occur and even the simple symptoms of physical dependence are exactly the same in both conditions: for example, weakness, dizziness while standing, nausea and trembling.

It should, however, be realized that when we talk about the problem of alcoholism we do not limit ourselves to those people who have developed such severe symptoms as those of *physical dependence on alcohol.* These occur in people whose consumption of alcohol is heaviest and is usually spread over a long period of time. This is not always so, for experimental evidence suggests that these physical symptoms may be developed quite quickly, provided large quantities of alcohol are consumed. In other words, as in the case of drugs, the symptoms are *dose-related.* If the problems of alcoholism were limited only to those people who showed symptoms of physical dependence, the problems would be much less extensive in numbers and simpler to identify.

It is not surprising, therefore, that large numbers of researchers into alcoholism have attempted to define the characteristics of what we may call abnormal drinking, for there is reason to believe that abnormal attitudes to alcohol lead to abnormal drinking behaviour and thus to alcoholism. As we have seen, Jellinek described five basic patterns of alcoholism. This classification, though helpful in many respects, is not entirely satisfactory since it may be regarded as an attempt to categorize alcohol-users in too rigid a way. Putting alcohol-users into watertight compartments may result in overlooking those people who have problems with alcohol but who cannot be fitted exactly into these groupings.

The symptoms of physical dependence on alcohol are fairly easy to spot and Jellinek has enumerated the main points. They include such symptoms as the development of shakes, that is attacks of uncontrollable shaking after drinking bouts, a feeling that drinking cannot be controlled, sleep disturbance, loss of appetite, and the fact that the drinker takes alcohol early in the day or in the morning to relieve a hangover. Further symptoms include blackouts and temporary losses of memory. Dramatic events such as *delirium tremens* and fits are easily recognized. Jellinek and others have laid emphasis on the fact that one of the earliest symptoms that indicate the onset of alcoholism is the loss of control a person may show in connection with his drinking habits. This loss of control is often a sign that the individual is becoming psychologically dependent on alcohol and his personal and social life is affected accordingly. This symptom is therefore an important development and one that needs to be recognized early.

It has been repeatedly pointed out that neither the drinker nor his friends are likely to recognize that the "loss of control stage" has been reached. The drinker uses various stratagems to deceive himself that his drinking is *not* getting out of control and he also tries to conceal from others any disturbing changes in himself. He may lie to himself and others about the amount he drinks, he may drink in large gulps so as to achieve the effect of alcohol as quickly as possible, and he may resort to devices such as taking extra drinks before going to parties or before encountering personal ordeals. He is constantly in a state of disquiet about the possibility of running out of alcohol, and he makes sure that there is always a supply in the house, in the office and even on his person when he goes out. Thus the alcoholic is not merely someone whose drinking has got out of hand; this habit has become the dominating feature of his existence. Through it he is creating within himself anxieties, fears, and misgivings about the possible outcome of his drinking habits, and is also beginning to create very real problems in his life in general. He is unable to cope with life effectively without increasing his intake of alcohol throughout the day.

The central question, which as yet remains unanswered, is

A protest against alcohol: a "Band of Hope" march through Westminster

whether alcoholism can be regarded as a unidimensional disorder or as a multidimensional one; that is to say, does every alcoholic suffer from exactly the same disorder which can be pinpointed somewhere along a line stretching from abstinence at one end to total preoccupation with alcohol at the other end? Or does the term alcoholism indicate a disorder which may have many factors in its causation relating to the person's psychological make-up, his sociocultural setting and his general background – as well as to the substance alcohol itself? The evidence to date is somewhat conflicting though modern thinking favours the latter (*multi-dimensional*) view of alcoholism.

There are good reasons for this since general clinical and social experience provides us with a series of examples of people who remain heavy habitual drinkers for a lifetime without developing any discernible disorder. These are often people whose consumption is in excess of those regarded as alcoholic. On the other hand one encounters people whose consumption may not appear excessive but which for them is too much and, what is more, has got out of control. This shows how important it is to appreciate the individual differences that occur in people.

Another fundamental question is whether there may be in some people a form of genetic or inherited defect which makes them less able than their fellows to deal with alcohol.

In recent years workers in Chile (Cruz-Coke, 1965, 1966) have suggested that there might be a genetically-determined link between alcoholism and colour-blindness. The authors suggest that since colour-blindness is a genetically-determined condition, the finding of an association between alcoholism and colour-blindness would lend support to the notion that alcoholism might in itself be a disorder with some genetic basis, for example possibly a fault in alcohol metabolism.

The Chileans apparently demonstrated such an association in the series on which they reported. However, there have been many criticisms of these findings, and even absolute rebuttals. The criticism was also made that the definition of alcoholism used in the Chilean studies was under suspicion. Since then it has not been possible for American and British workers to link the incidence of alcoholism and colour-blindness in any of their own researches.

Evidence for the genetic inheritance of alcoholism in family and twin studies has to date been rather inconclusive. At present the consensus of opinion is that no case has been made for genetic predisposition to alcoholism. An alternative view, frequently found in the literature on the subject, emphasizes the importance of childhood experience in encouraging people into alcoholism in later life, for example under the influence of parents who are themselves alcoholic. Unfortunately this view is difficult to maintain since it cannot always be established clearly whether or not the parents were themselves alcoholic. The evidence may be based on retrospective surveys, which are a well known source of error. However, at least one important inquiry should be mentioned. This is the Cambridge – Somerville Youth Study described by the McCords (1960).

The McCords were involved in a prospective study of some hundreds of young people at a Community Psychiatric Centre in Cambridge, Massachusetts. This started in 1935 and their observations on this group of youngsters together with a control group formed the basis not only for their publications on the origin of alcoholism but for their work on the origins of delinquent behaviour. These youngsters were followed up over a twenty-year period. The McCords traced over 500 of the original youngsters and were able to establish the percentage who had become problem drinkers. They attempted to relate their subsequent alcoholism to the initial observations that had been made on the youngsters at the beginning of the study.

Some doubt has been raised as to the soundness of the criteria they used for the diagnosis of alcoholism. For instance, if an individual had been arrested for drunkenness more than twice or had been treated for drink problems this was thought to indicate alcoholism.

Using such evidence as diagnostic of alcoholism, at least 10 per cent of the people investigated were regarded as alcoholic. This is of interest because at the time when the follow-up was carried out the subjects were still relatively young. Nevertheless there is a great deal of information in the report which reinforces other findings described elsewhere in American Alcoholics and it is perhaps not surprising that the most reliable information is concerned with factors relating to the incidence of alcoholism. For instance, United-States-born Americans, Western European, and Irish-Americans showed a significantly higher rate of alcoholism than that shown by Italians and other Latin-American people.

The presence of obvious family discord about drinking is a bad sign, and, in general, a family atmosphere which includes such disturbances as illegitimacy and incestuous relations is thought to have an unhealthy influence on the later development of alcoholism.

The authors drew further attention to the possible relevance of poor relationships between parents, and the possible role of the mother. Now there is little doubt that disturbed relationships between parents and children are common in families with alcohol problems. The difficulty is to know how much weight to give to them, for much the same incidence of intra-familial disturbances has been found in drug-users and, for that matter in people with unclassified psychiatric disorders. In a study carried out by the author (1969, 1970) in which United Kingdom heroin-users were compared with United States heroin-users a large number of similarities were found in the two groups. These similarities related to the incidence of disturbed family relationships, psychiatric disorders in the family, alcoholism and so on. Perhaps more important was the associated findings that when the drug-using groups were compared with a matched group of patients receiving treatment in psychiatric hospitals for conditions unrelated to drugs or alcohol, the psychiatric patients had very similar backgrounds of family disturbance, parental alcoholism, etc., to the members of the drug-using groups. Further, all three groups had a much higher incidence of these disturbances than a control group.

It should be emphasized that in the study of human behaviour the findings of the observers rarely tie up with the expectations of theorists. At the present time attempts to explain the development of alcoholism in general on the basis of one particular theory appear to be less than satisfactory and the multidimensional theory of alcoholism is likely, in the long run, to be a more helpful line of inquiry. The "unidimensional" theory categorizes people as being either alcoholic or non-alcoholic and assumes that "alcoholism" is a single behavioural trait. However, doubt has been cast on this notion by many authorities.

Wanberg (1969) commented that to date few attempts had been made to identify the greatly-differing patterns of drinking that may occur in a recognized population of alcoholics. However, in a certain investigation over two thousand known alcoholics were interviewed and it was found that there were as many as thirteen individual patterns of drinking, although it was conceded that these drinking patterns were interrelated.

Another investigation included an attempt to relate different drinking symptoms to five general classifications connected with the "use of drink for stated purposes." Among the conclusions it was found that two main attitudes existed in the majority of the subjects; these were the claim that people "drink to relax" and the admission to feelings of shame about conduct under the influence of alcohol. Five symptoms were found to be moderately prevalent. These included morning drinking, shakes, blackouts and vague feelings of fear and anxiety after drinking bouts. Since a considerable variation of symptoms resulting from drinking was found amongst established alcoholics it appears that alcoholism is a multidimensional-type disorder. Common sense would surely support such an observation. It would be most unlikely that every person who becomes alcoholic follows an identical pattern. What we call "alcoholism" should properly be defined in medical terms as a "syndrome," that is to say a constellation of signs and symptoms which help us to name a disorder without being able to define its causation. A syndrome may have many causes. The continued study of human behaviour demonstrates repeatedly that theories of causation based on the "all the eggs in one basket" or "omnium gatherum" principle are likely to be fallacious.

A further tantalizing question about alcoholism remains: is the alcoholic likely to develop some form of permanent change in his bodily biochemistry which renders him less able to deal with alcohol, less able to control his intake and therefore more prone to go on drinking in a pathological way? This can occur with a minority of alcoholics whose physical dependence is so great as to be followed by loss of tolerance associated with liver damage. Such a condition has the further effect of reducing their ability to metabolize alcohol and hence of becoming more vulnerable to alcohol and uncontrolled drinking. But such alcoholics are a minority in an extensive and poorly comprehended group.

Chapter 6

Causes of drug-dependence and alcoholism: some personal factors

It seems likely that important causative factors of dependence are in some way related to the individual's personality and its development. Some people have a history of difficulty in coping with life in general, are unable to form satisfactory and stable relationships with others and seem to have a tendency to drift into antisocial behaviour. Besides this they seem to need the special gratifications that illicit drug-use or intemperate alcohol-use may provide. In such cases we tend to regard drug-dependence, alcoholism or persistent delinquency as the result of some disorder of the individual's personality. This is not to suggest that *all* alcoholics or drug-users have personality disorders but merely to state the role of personality disorder in this condition. A good deal of research has been carried out into the possible relevance of individual personality factors in the development of dependence, and some notable studies will be reviewed here. Before attempting this it is appropriate to examine at least three key terms. Personality, Personality Disorder and Psychopathic Personality.

Since people with severe drug or alcohol problems frequently have personality disorders it is fair to start by asking what is meant by the term *personality*. Not every reader will necessarily have a clear idea of the meaning of this often loosely-used word.

Personality *is* hard to define, and indeed many definitions have been put forward, but there is at least a consensus of agreement about its meaning amongst behavioural scientists. Perhaps the areas of dispute arise mainly from the fact that different writers are inclined to lay stress on different aspects of the structure and development of the personality. At all events a definition that might win fairly general acceptance is that the term means the sum total of an individual's characteristics: attributes and behaviour.

Many attempts have been made to classify or categorize human personality and we have to ask how personality can be assessed, as the term appears to cover rather ephemeral concepts. Most psychologists would admit that the assessment is not easy since our understanding of personality structure and development is far from clear and our methods fall far short of any acceptable scientific standard.

The earliest attempts to classify personality were those we call "descriptive," that is, those based on straightforward observations of human behaviour. A typology of personality would be constructed using rather obvious distinctions (with less obvious sources of error) such as clever . . . stupid, jolly . . . sad. The disadvantage of this descriptive approach is its lack of precision – it does not measure what it is supposed to – and its unreliability, for it cannot be repeated with any degree of accuracy.

Other attempts at classifying personality start from the hypothesis that personality has an underlying framework of a dimensional sort – that is to say that attributes and behavioural characteristics can be measured by their position on a continuum – each continuum representing a polarity of attributes, for example, introversion . . . extraversion.

Another view stresses the importance of unconscious forces in shaping the personality and moulding it into a recognizable whole. This "psychodynamic" model emphasizes the role of childhood experience, relationships with parents and unconscious conflicts in colouring the personality.

Other psychological theories point to one particular aspect of behaviour as contributing primarily to the development of personality. Behavioural psychologists emphasize the importance of the learning process, while others suggest that the development of a man's personality is conditioned by the concepts that he forms of the world around him.

Whatever theories are held, whatever methods of assessment are employed, there is pretty general agreement that there is such a condition as a personality disorder.

The term *personality disorder* is applied to people in whom there is clear evidence of abnormal behaviour and abnormal life experience from an early age, where this persists and is not a change in behaviour or experience such as is found in a person developing a psychiatric illness.

The concept of personality disorder or "abnormal personality" has been made difficult to understand by the use of the term "psychopathic personality," a term often used to describe persistent abnormalities of conduct which are frequently antisocial and do damage both to the person and to society. There is no doubt that this term has been misused and misapplied.

A good definition of *psychopathic personality* was provided by the German psychiatrist Schneider, who defined psychopaths as "those abnormal personalities who suffer from their abnormality or cause society to suffer."

RELATIONSHIP OF DRUG–DEPENDENCE AND ALCOHOLISM TO PREVIOUSLY EXISTING PSYCHIATRIC DISORDERS

If drug-dependence and alcoholism are to be regarded as psychological illnesses in their own right we would not be surprised to find a higher incidence of straightforward psychiatric disorders among drug-users. We would expect the drug-user to be more vulnerable to psychiatric illness than the average person. In fact, however, there is no real evidence that this is so. On the other hand only a small proportion of drug-users and people with alcohol problems develop in this way as a result of their own symptoms and the accidental discovery that drugs or alcohol will give relief.

PERSONAL FACTORS: RELATIONSHIP OF DRUG–DEPENDENCE TO PERSONALITY DISORDERS

As we have said, many people who become dependent on drugs have personality disorders and this is because those with abnormal personalities are more vulnerable to drug-dependence than the "normal" person.

A word here about the use of the word "normal" will not be out of place. It is often said that psychologists and psychiatrists spend so much of their time with "sick" or "abnormal" people that they are not able to distinguish the "normal" from the "abnormal." The question "How *can* you tell the abnormal from the normal?" is often asked. The answer to this is not so difficult as people suppose. When psychologists and psychiatrists talk about "abnormal" people they use the term in a statistical sense. They are referring to those people who differ markedly from the average. This may be illustrated by a simple example. If one were to measure the height of everyone in the population and plot numbers according to height, the graph would show that the bulk of the population occupies the centre of the range and the extremes (representing giants and dwarfs) are occupied by a very small proportion. In statistics, this kind of distribution is called a "normal" distribution.

For the behavioural scientist the term "normal" means characteristic of the bulk of the population. The "abnormal" are those who deviate markedly from the commonly-accepted modes and standards of feeling, behaviour and perception. Used in this way "normal" and "abnormal" are acceptable and useful terms.

It is sometimes said to be impossible to assess the personality of a drug-user since the effects of the drug itself will have altered his personality. Most of the studies made of the personality of drug-users relate to those who use opiates; however, experimental and clinical work has so far given no evidence to support the suggestion that the taking of opiates changes the personality. This may seem implausible but while we know that drugs *can* alter behaviour, we also know that a person's behaviour under the influence of drugs is altered in the short term rather than the long term.

We have to concede, nevertheless, that since present methods of personality assessment are less than adequate these statements may possibly be qualified at some future time. After all, psychology and psychiatry are now only at the stage of development which general science reached as long ago as the eighteenth century.

Literature on the relationship between personality disorders and drug-dependence is diverse and extensive, and it is clearly beyond the scope of this work to review it completely. Certain studies, however, deserve examination, as they give some information about the way in which people become dependent on drugs as a result of personality problems. Before examining these in any detail it is worth looking at possible sources of error to help our interpretation.

Most of the studies have been carried out in institutions. Now the observer in an institution, despite his claims to scientific credibility, is likely to be influenced by serious prejudices.

People who work in an institution, whether as staff members or even as "independent" researchers, can unconsciously be influenced by the atmosphere of the place to the extent of expecting inmates to behave in ways which will confirm their presuppositions. This may sound fanciful but has been noticed by many authorities (for example, Goffman, 1954; Lindesmith, 1965). Again people studied in an institutional setting may well represent the most abnormal sector of a population affected by behavioural disturbance, whether it be drug-taking, delinquency or whatever. The drug-user in hospital or prison is likely to be someone with greater disability than the one who remains in the community. The ability to cope in the community, to stay out of hospital and out of prison implies a greater degree of personal and psychological organization than is shown by someone who is institutionalized. The institutional population therefore gives rise to bias, both because of the selection of subjects and because of influences acting on the observer.

Having said this it is only fair to add that research-workers whether their area of study be human behaviour, plant taxonomy, or for that matter the life-cycle of the great crested grebe, can only study subjects made available to them, and so far research-workers in the United States and in the United Kingdom have had access only to people in institutions.

Fortunately in recent years, in the United Kingdom, there have also been a number of reports about people studied in the community (Kosviner *et al.*, 1958; D'Alarcon *et al.*, 1969). Studying people in the community is difficult. Contact with them may be fleeting and they may be reluctant to co-operate in prolonged investigations, particularly if their life-style has illicit associations. A fruitful line of research might well be to follow up very carefully those drug-dependent patients who have never been in either prison or hospital. Unhappily it has to be acknowledged that their numbers – if one judges from patients attending clinics – may be small, but this may simply reflect the possibility that clinics deal with the "worst" cases.

With these points in mind it will now perhaps be of value to examine some of the studies carried out on the personalities of drug-users.

Most of the psychological researches in this area deal with two main topics: firstly attempts to explore the dynamics of drug-usage, that is the unconscious forces and processes which may cause a person to use drugs, and secondly attempts to identify possible personality types relating to groups of drug-users.

Perhaps it would be appropriate to start with an opposing point of view extracted from the comments of Lindesmith (1949, 1956, 1965). This American sociologist has questioned the existence of what he calls "the addiction-prone" personality on the fundamental basis that there have been such apparent discrepancies between the reputed "personality types" of drug-users as to cast serious doubt on the validity of the concept.

As an alternative he states a general theory of drug-dependence which emphasizes the *craving* of the drug-taker and postulates that the *craving* is "generated in the repetition of using drugs to relieve withdrawal distress, provided that this distress is properly understood by the user." Lindesmith is very careful to emphasize that this theory does *not* mean that someone who is dependent on drugs is so because of a process of self-recognition, as if he woke up one day and realized that relieving symptoms with drugs meant he was an addict. Rather he means that the drug-user repeatedly lives through, learns and forms a concept of the experience – the distressing experience of abstinence, so that he then learns and moves into the subjective experience and life style of a drug-user.

Lindesmith has referred to this as "cognitive conditioning." Thus one might say that a drug-user does not become a drug-user by proclaiming himself to be so but by his learning that he is one.

Lindesmith takes issue with the generally-accepted view that dependence is an outgrowth of major personality disorders. Indeed, he goes further than this and suggests that if people selected at random were given regular doses of opiate-type drugs for a time all of them would become dependent on the drug "irrespective of personality, character, social class or motives." This assertion is unanswerable and the proposition untestable. It should be remarked, however, that thousands of people do receive repeated doses of opiates in medical treatment and neither wish to repeat or continue the experience nor become dependent.

Reviewing the possible role of personality disorder in drug-dependence, Lindesmith (1965) made pithy comments about the wide range of findings described. He produced a list of the personality types of drug-users culled from the literature, including the following: "alienated, aggressive psychopath, childlike, cyclothymic, constitutionally immoral, emotionally unstable, extroverted, dependent, essentially normal, frustrated, hostile, hereditarily neuropathic, hedonistic, introspective, infantile, inebriate, lack of moral sense, motivational immaturity, nomadic, narcissistic, neurasthenic, pseudo-psychopathic delinquent, passive psychopath, paranoid, sociopathic, self-indulgent, self-conscious, weak character and will." He points out that many of these terms contradict each other and that some are meaningless, though he spares the authors concerned the embarrassment of being named. He also notes that when large-scale studies have been carried out on socially-disorganized groups such as vagrants and recidivist prisoners the same list of epithets have been applied to them. In other words, such categories may well be inadequate ways of describing people who continually fail to match up to the expectations of society.

He regards such "categories" as being the effect of drug-taking and drug-dependence on a person's ability to survive in contemporary society. He adds that these categorical epithets can often be used as barely concealed expressions of disapproval.

Lindesmith's criticisms highlight many of the basic methodological flaws that are found in certain studies and also the intuitive approach that characterizes much of the writing on this complex topic.

If the attempt is made, however, not so much to label the personalities of drug-users – a dubious procedure anyway – but rather to evaluate the person concerned in the context of his previous life-history, early development, etc. (that is, a biography, not a snapshot) it should be possible to show whether or not a population of drug-users is significantly deviant in carefully-defined terms.

Again the long-term effects of drugs can be evaluated and, if necessary, discarded as irrelevant. Since it can be argued that alcohol or prolonged vagrancy could have had the same effects that Lindesmith has attributed to drugs, it may be that personality disorder determines the choice of a way of life rather than anything so specific as a drug-dependent state. In other words a socially-deviant person is likely to choose drug-usage for what it offers as a life-style rather than for its "pure" drug aspects.

While a non-deviant or "normal" person might become dependent on a drug when given repeated injections, he is less likely to choose the life of a drug-dependent, given the ordinary course of events, unless obliged to do so by some other important factor such as a chronic painful illness. The "normal" person gets no gratification from taking illicit drugs, or from a "drug" way of life and has no need to join a deviant subculture.

Lindesmith's view is not shared by Wikler whose researches into opiate-dependence are authoritative and based on personally-conducted experiments. His objections to Lindesmith's position are as follows: that, first of all, people who are dependent on opiates show persistent disorders of mood even when they have access to unlimited supplies of the drug (a view which the present author's experience would confirm); secondly, that painless reduction of opiate drugs and total withdrawal is easily accomplished; and thirdly that tolerance to the variety of special pleasure or euphoria caused by opiates is quickly developed and these are rarely repeated as intensely by a given person despite increases in dosage.

There is one very detailed and frequently quoted study, that was carried out by Wikler (1952) in which a middle-aged male morphine-user was experimentally re-addicted to morphine and allowed to regulate his own dosage in hospital in a controlled situation. He was studied during abstinences during the first and last two months of his dependence, and over a period of reduction and withdrawal. Most of the study is concerned with interviews carried out with the patient, but on the basis of his observations, admittedly of one patient, the author put forward a number of tentative propositions about possible unconscious processes that relate to drug-dependence. He suggests that experiences following the injection of morphine are related to the direct gratification of what he calls "primary needs," that is, relief of hunger, fear, pain and sexual urges. He casts doubt on the use of the terms "normal" and "euphoria" when applied to drug-users, since he believes that the drug-dependent person who uses opiates achieves primary gratification from the drug because it damps down these basic primary needs. He goes on to suggest that when tolerance to morphia is developed and the user loses these gratifications, they are replaced by new sources of gratification which are associated in time with the development of physical dependence which itself replaces the original primary needs and which can only be satisfied by drug-use.

Wikler casts doubt on the idea that a search for pleasurable experience underlies the tendency to relapse, whatever drug-users may say, since this would imply that drug-users recall only the first pleasant doses of the drug and forget the miseries they endure during the period of drug-dependence. Physical dependence on the drug becomes linked by conditioning to life-situations, often of an everyday sort, which are associated with the availability of drugs, and situations in which withdrawal symptoms have previously been experienced. An example in the present author's experience is of a man who, after serving a five-year prison sentence, went down a street where he used to obtain illicit supplies of heroin and speedily developed withdrawal sickness and pains.

Wikler's views on the causes of drug-dependence tend to be behaviouristic, that is to say they belong to that school of psychology which sees human behaviour not in "mentalistic" or subjective terms, but as the product of a learning-process developed by conditioning. Wikler believes that physical dependence develops on a similar basis to classical Pavlovian conditioning, that is through the association in time of a particular environment with the experience of withdrawal symptoms. Drug-seeking is reinforced and intensified by repeated reduction of abstinence-distress when the user is able to obtain more drugs between doses. There has been some experimental verification of this theory in research on rats. Wikler (1962) used Etonitazene (a substance unrelated to morphine but 1,000 times more potent than morphine as a pain-reliever) in a series of experiments. He and co-workers were able to show that conditioned physical withdrawal symptoms could develop in rats long after they had become abstinent from this substance.

RELATIONSHIP OF THE "SOCIALLY DEVIANT PERSONALITY" TO DRUG DEPENDENCE

This was reviewed and discussed by Hill (1962) who examined various hypothesis and research possibilities in drug-dependence. Hill's main interest in this review lies in his previously reported findings of evidence for the presence of *social deviance* in the personalities of drug-users. His view is that in the United States, at any rate, alcoholics and drug-users, studied in groups, show social deviance as a common predominant personality characteristic and that this is likely to have existed long before they became involved with either drugs or alcohol. Much of Hill's work in this area has involved the use of the MMPI – Minnesota Multiphasic Personality Inventory. The MMPI is a questionnaire test containing several hundred questions which has been used since the 1940s as a personality test.

It contains nine basic clinical scales based on the replies to the questionnaire. Each clinical scale is named after a clinical psychiatric state such as depression, hysteria, etc., on the assumption that a number of appropriate answers to a given scale will indicate a person who is either suffering from the condition named (in the case of high scores) or at least presents the elements of that condition, or something resembling it, in his personality structure. In practice the MMPI scales also have some relevance to the "healthy" person, since answers to the questionnaire provide a profile type picture of the elements in any individual's make-up. Like most psychological tests, however, this is subject to basic criticism as regards its reliability and validity (that is, is it right and is it repeatable?). Most psychologists would agree that the results of such a test are only acceptable when examined in the light of the results of a number of other tests carried out on the same person. In other words you cannot judge, estimate, gauge or assess a person until you know a good deal about him.

It is interesting to note that in the MMPI there is one scale, the Pd or Psychopathic Deviate scale which is regarded as measuring *social deviance.* Hill postulates that when we define someone as socially deviant we are implying that he does not share the commonly-accepted needs, motives, aspirations, goals and aims of the bulk of his fellows. His chief finding in repeated studies on drug-users is a consistent high rating on the Pd scale, suggesting that drug-dependent people share a common trait of social deviancy. He has reviewed very interestingly the various ways in which the socially-deviant person may be more vulnerable to drug-usage than his less deviant fellows. He suggests that the factors which may develop this increased vulnerability in the deviant person are first of all his basic deficiency in the ordinary social pursuits which society regards as acceptable and which might themselves exert a socializing influence on him. Secondly, he reinforces an observation already recorded, that socially-deviant people tend to show little guilt or anxiety about the social consequences of their acts. This may appear to state the obvious, but we have to remember that one of the functions of research is to verify anecdote and the intuitive deductions of common sense.

Further information on the possible relationship between personality structure and opiate-use has been given by Gerard and Kornetsky (1955), Chein *et al.* (1964) and Chein (1965).

Gerard and Kornetsky (1955) presented the hypotheses later developed by Chein *et al.* (1964), that people who live in areas where illicit opiate use is endemic are unlikely to become dependent on opiates unless they show evidence of existing psychological disturbance. The authors state that "becoming an addict is a highly-individualized process that can only be understood in the context of the individual's personality structure, past life situation and present interaction with the significant figures of his familial and peer groups."

This complex view of drug-use as a personal and social problem was more extensively developed in the publications of Chein *et al.* (1964). In an earlier work Gerard and Kornetsky (1954) had studied a group of thirty-two adolescent male heroin-users and concluded that there appeared to be a relationship between the drug-dependent state and pre-existing personality disorders. This was an interesting report because it was probably one of the first that drew attention to the phenomenon of "dysphoria" – a mood of depressive pessimism and low self-regard often found in drug-users. All the subjects in this series showed dysphoria and a disordered awareness of their own sexuality, also poor ability to maintain stable relationships with others. There was some suggestion that their mothers might have played a key role in the causation of their personality problems, although in the present author's view evidence for this was inconclusive.

These observations received further support from the work of Chein *et al.* (1964) which reported a study of drug-using youngsters and non-drug-using youngsters in New York City. In their now classic work, Chein and his colleagues made many pertinent comments, including the observation that the problems of drug-usage are frequently viewed in "distorted perspective" (a timely reminder), and that there is little real evidence that narcotic

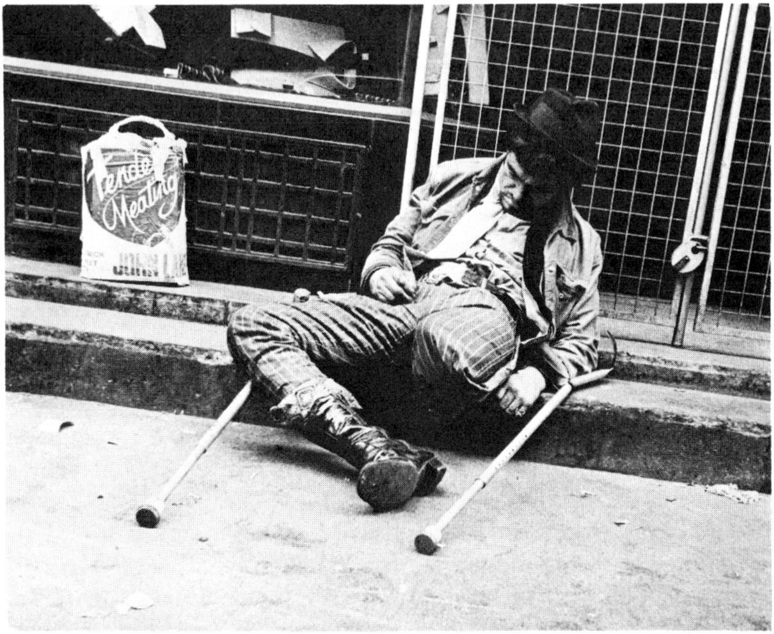

An extreme case of the consequences of using unsterilized needles for self-injection

use is intrinsically damaging, either physically or psychologically. This latter is a contentious statement. Narcotics may and do cause damage by second-order effects – from dirty syringes, etc. – and it is perhaps disingenuous to exclude narcotics from blame on this account. After all, very few diabetics die of septicaemia The authors also rightly comment that the relationship between drug-use and delinquency is not a simple one. They postulate a typology of drug-dependence which discounts the over-inclusiveness of a procedure that would classify someone as "just an addict."

Perhaps most important is the way in which these authors drew attention to the epidemiology of drug-use in New York, its incidence, prevalence and mode of spread. They made shrewd observations on the social and economic associations of drug-misuse. In general their findings were concerned with "ghetto" or "near ghetto" dwellers and their general conclusion was that although heroin-use in New York City was, in some unspecified way, associated with life in areas of economic squalor, ultimately other factors as well as social and economic ones operated – although they could not demonstrate the precise nature of these factors. They remark that the youngster who becomes a drug-user in New York is likely to have grown up in an area where real material loss and lack of identification with a reliable adult are the rule. Also the authors comment shrewdly on the natural history of drug-use and name four stages of dependence – viz., experimentation, occasional use, regular use and efforts to break the habit.

As to the possible role of personality disorders in drug-dependence Chein *et al.* (1964) claimed that these disorders are not to be regarded as a consequence of drug-use. They put forward five hypotheses about the personality development of the drug-user and its moulding in the family. These are:

1 That a person who becomes drug-dependent is likely to have weak ego structure. His ability to direct his own energies, aspirations, and so on is poor.
2 That such a person would be likely to show "defective super-ego functioning," that is a lack of constraints on his behaviour deriving from normal emotional development.
3 That he or she would show inadequate identification in the masculine or feminine role.
4 That he would show a lack of realistic orientation towards the future.
5 That he would show a mistrust of major social institutions, police, education, law enforcement.

It should perhaps be said here that the fifth hypothesis receives little support from a study of young New York heroin-users. At the time of the study such people were likely to be slum-dwellers, Negros or Puerto Ricans, people for whom a distrust of major social institutions might almost be called normal.

The authors also suggested that the family backgrounds of such youngsters were apt to encourage such development. By using highly-detailed structured interviews in the families, itemizing them and analysing the results statistically, the authors were able to produce convincing evidence that their subjects' family backgrounds had made such a contribution.

This kind of study is easily criticized on the grounds that it is inherently likely to demonstrate what it sets out to prove by the very nature of its design, by using biased questions and questions based on unverifiable assumptions. This is probably too glib a criticism. One might concede the difficulties of defining exactly "weak ego structure" and "defective super-ego functioning," but nevertheless, within their own self-imposed limits, the authors' researches give useful supporting evidence to the proposition that the drug-users they studied had personality disorders before they took up drugs. Also there runs through the whole work a note of humane non-assertive common sense which is both refreshing and inspiring.

In a clinical and social study of adolescent opiate-addicts, Gerard and Kornetsky (1954), reported their findings about a group of adolescent heroin-users. Clearly there are reservations about the value of case-reports. After all, this kind of study relates to people who are in difficulties and who are likely to be abnormal; but one cannot write off such researches, and this one shows all the signs of honest recording and unprejudiced discussion.

The main findings concerned the subjects' psychiatric disabilities. The authors tried to apply a diagnostic classification to the people studied, noting that generally there was demonstrated a common pattern of diminished self-esteem, pessimism about the future and a general tendency to aimlessness and lack of purpose. They commented on sexual immaturity in the subjects and a history of poor ability to form and maintain stable relationships with others. The authors named four personality types which they diagnosed and, in a later study, they compared a group of adolescent heroin-users and controls. In this later report they employed not only clinical interviews but fairly extensive psychological testing. The types of personality disorder reported on in both papers included:

1 Overt schizophrenia
2 Incipient schizophrenia
3 Delinquency-dominated character (personality) disorders
4 Inadequate personalities

Now, without going into the diagnostic niceties of these reports, we can comment that overall the drug-users showed a striking incidence of these "personality disorders" as compared with the controls. This evidence may not clinch the theory but it does lend it support. We may quibble about the use of terms such as schizophrenia in this context, but perhaps we may draw the general conclusion that the drug-users in this series were *predominantly* people who showed evidence of personality disturbance before drug-use. The label given to this abnormality is in a sense irrelevant. They were in fact disorganized and unhappy people before they started to take drugs.

The authors' general conclusion was clear and simple. They said that their findings "supported the hypothesis that young men living in an area where illicit drug-use was widespread were unlikely to become addicted to drugs independently of pre-existing psychiatric disturbances within their own personality development." They concluded that drug-dependence was a "highly individualized process which could only be understood in the context of the persons involved, their personality structure, past life history, and present interactions with the important figures of their families and peer groups." To some no doubt these comments were self-evident, but it should be recalled that even into the 1950s too much of the literature about drug-users was moralizing, overstated and oversimple. The authors made penetrating comments about the lack of self-esteem in adolescent drug-users and linked this attribute to the general quality of their lives beforehand, noting the "prevalence of façades of indifference covering self-doubt and self-distrust."

It may be felt that the findings of this type of study are not applicable to subjects studied in the United Kingdom. This is fair comment. One cannot transpose conclusions from one culture to another. But even accepting sensibly the cultural differences between United States and United Kingdom drug-users we can predict that United Kingdom drug-users are likely to show major areas of personality disorder. Many studies of hospitalized patients in this country bear out this prediction (Bewley, 1966; James, 1969; Willis, 1968, 1969). We can at least say that when heroin-users in the United Kingdom are studied in hospital they are more likely than not to show a history of early personality disturbance. We cannot be so certain about the misusers of drugs such as the amphetamines, or alcohol. Alcoholics are a much more heterogeneous population.

A recent large-scale study of personality structure and its possible relationship to drug-abuse has been reported by Cockett

(1971). This investigation was carried out in a Remand Centre in England where the author and his colleagues carried out extensive social and psychological inquiries into the background and personalities of young male offenders – over 2,500 in all. After a preliminary investigation involving 563 subjects the main part of this research examined the psychological and social attributes of a sample of over 400 drug-users drawn from 1,577 young offenders who were on remand in the centre concerned.

Drug-using offenders were carefully matched against non-drug-using offenders in respect of age and social background, and detailed comparisons were made. The comparisons involved the use of detailed batteries of psychological tests and structured questionnaires which examined their social backgrounds with particular reference to educational and work histories, family structure, criminality and patterns of drug-usage.

There were a number of interesting findings. Drug-usage was found to be a "generalized characteristic rather than one related to specific drug substances." The history of the individual's in volvement with drug-use was found to be a very relevant aspect of drug-taking – crucial in any attempt to understand the natural history of drug-usage. Over 20 per cent of the subjects had discontinued drug use. This finding should not cause surprise; to date follow-up studies carried out in the United States suggest a natural remission rate of the order of 20 – 30 per cent. Perhaps the most interesting finding was that family disruption was, in general, unrelated to drug-taking when drug-taking offenders are compared with non-drug-taking offenders, for as will have been realized, family disruption is usually accorded a high relevance in the "causation" of drug-dependence. In fact in Crockett's study the drug-users showed a lower incidence of disturbed family backgrounds than did non-drug-using offenders.

Poor work records were found to show a clear association with drug-use and there was absolutely no evidence to suggest that the possession of either high or low intelligence influenced a person towards drug-use.

The investigation of the personality structure of drug-users involved not only detailed batteries of tests but also the statistical analysis of test results. These were used in an attempt to identify factors which might contribute to a personality type that could be regarded as unduly vulnerable to drug-dependence.

Summarizing his findings the author commented that the results represented the outcome of testing a mixed group of offenders of whom two-thirds were psychiatrically normal and one-third abnormal and that they varied in their involvement in drug-use "from non-users to the addicted." The analysis of factors involved in the personality of the "typical" drug-user suggested that such an individual could be regarded as rather an insecure person – someone with a poorly integrated personality, likely to be hypochondriacal in his attitudes towards physical symptoms and generally rather radical and non-moralizing in his social attitudes – attitudes which the author does not implicitly condemn but rather highlights as being part of a matrix of socio-cultural constructs – a view of the world, one might say, of which as observers we can only be aware.

INDIVIDUAL FACTORS: THE EFFECTS OF DRUGS ON MOOD

There is no doubt that many substances do cause an elevation of mood (euphoria). The list includes not only opiates but barbiturates, cocaine, cannabis, alcohol, aspirin, and even coffee and anti-freeze. But what is surprising is that substances with such differing properties can produce such similar effects, not only in an individual but in groups of people.

Wikler (1952), commenting on drug effects on mood, distinguished between three types of drug-induced pleasure. First he noted that opiates may act by gratifying primary needs (as previously described) whilst alcohol, barbiturates, amphetamines and cannabis do not gratify such needs. Secondly, he suggested that these latter drugs reduce a person's control of the emotional mechanisms they have developed to relieve "secondary" emotional needs. He regards this as a distinguishing factor between opiates and other drugs. Thirdly, he comments on a possible effect which *all* these drugs share if taken in large enough doses, namely the reduction of a person's awareness of problems which normally would cause anxiety. Acknowledging this he nevertheless remarks on the difficulties involved in trying to separate the euphoric effect of a drug from the taker's situation and circumstances when he takes it. This is a theme which constantly recurs in studies on the effects of drugs on people.

PARTICULAR EFFECTS OF DRUGS ON BEHAVIOUR AND THINKING – THEIR RELATION TO PERSONAL CAUSES IN DRUG-DEPENDENCE

In general it has been found that dependency-producing drugs cause two varieties of change in people's behaviour. Firstly those changes which are related to the person's previous experience and personality structure, and secondly those changes which are perhaps more predictable and more directly related to drug action and which we can more easily regard as specific to the drug used.

It seems likely that the first type of change following drug-taking is what has been termed a "release effect." The drug causes a person to lose conscious control over his behaviour so that unusual acts become possible. This behaviour may be unacceptable to him and to society, even though it is part of his unconscious mental life. It is an interesting paradox that although

Drawing by an addict under treatment. The content of the picture suggests loneliness and isolation

an individual may experience elevation of mood after using a range of widely differing drugs, for example, cannabis, opiates or barbiturates, the changes in thought and fantasy may be very different in contents as also may be changes in behaviour. There is no consistency, therefore, between his elevated mood and other psychological changes that occur.

It is difficult to describe or understand the essential nature of the subjective experience that follows the use of drugs such as opiates. We cannot rely entirely on descriptions set down by creative literary geniuses who happen to have been opiate-users, since the imaginative perceptions of the creative artist are not necessarily shared by all. Also there is, in general, an understandable reluctance to indulge in self-experiment. At the same time, we are reluctant to accept fully the comments of the established drug-user on drug effects. He is often dishonest in talking about whole areas of his life, and we have no reason to expect him to be more truthful in his reports on drug effects.

There is good reason for believing that the drug-user exaggerates the pleasurable aspects of drug-taking. Many observations of opiate effects by regular users may be motivated by exhibitionist tendencies and the need to make out a strong case for getting more of the drug.

It is interesting to record, however, that traditional descriptions in medical literature may be just as misleading because of their recurrent tendency to assign a completely joyous or euphoric effect to drugs. These claims are not borne out by the study of their problematic subjective effects.

Reporting on the effects of drugs on mood, Lasagna *et al.* (1955) described a series of experiments in which attempts were made to assess the effects of opiates, amphetamine sulphate and a barbiturate. The people studied included twenty young healthy adult males, thirty sick patients and thirty "post-addicts." The post-addicts were all people with a history of hospital admissions and imprisonment for heroin- and morphine-addiction. All the subjects were carefully evaluated with structured interviews and questionnaires aimed at assessing their mood, level of wakefulness, ability to concentrate and also the possible side-effects of the drugs used. In fact the main object of the study was to find out whether the drugs involved produced a feeling of pleasure in the taker.

Thomas de Quincey, author of "Confessions of an English Opium- Eater"

"Euphoria" was said to be present if the taker described a state that was more pleasant than that which existed before the injection of the drug. The injections were given at spaced intervals in a way that would not reveal to the patient what he was re-receiving. The only consistently pleasure-producing drug in the series was amphetamine sulphate, whose effect was rarely described in neutral fashion by post-addicts or by normal subjects.

Perhaps one of the more interesting findings was that opiates produced an indifferent response in fifteen subjects who said that they had no wish to repeat the drug experience. Correct identification of the drugs used by post-addicts was uncommon. Normal subjects found that in general morphine and heroin were not pleasant drugs.

We therefore need to be sceptical when opiates are described as inevitably pleasure-producing substances. We have to remember that pleasure is not likely to be experienced without some cause. It will probably be experienced by someone with long-standing difficulties in obtaining any sort of interest in life and who is therefore highly motivated to use a drug which is reputed to be pleasure-giving and whose attractiveness may be heightened by its illicit associations.

An interesting instance of this occurred in New York after the Second World War when heroin-users took up a new type of heroin which they said gave a very good "high." Samples that were analysed turned out to be composed of milk sugar (lactose).

"LIFE-STYLE ADAPTATION"

It may well be that the unrelenting study of personality typology in drug-users will, in the end, turn out to be fruitless. This is the view put forward by Freedman and Brotman (1965) who suggest that a better line of inquiry is to concentrate on typologies of drug-use and relate drug use patterns to the life-styles adopted by users. They base their inquiry on what they have called "life-style adaption," since they feel that studies of personality have frequently been biased by the climate of general opinion. Such a climate can lead the researchers themselves unconsciously to use stereotyped ideas about the supposed characteristics of "typical drug-users." They took a sample of over 200 drug-users

A barbiturate-injector takes refuge in St. Anne's parish church in London's Soho

in a three-year period with no preconceptions about them. They commented that two opposing views had been prevalent in America. Early in the century they were viewed as dangerous criminals, a view which changed with the passage of time to one which saw the user as basically a rejected and dependent sick person in need of treatment. Although the latter view is a humane one it is likely to be as erroneous as the first. Both are too simple. It is likely that drug-users as a group are a heterogeneous population.

These workers have looked at general dimensions of behaviour in the drug-user, conventional as opposed to deviant behaviour, and criminality as opposed to non-criminality. Also they have examined the users' involvement with various sub-cultures which can be categorized along the lines "conventionality – deviancy" and "non-criminality – criminality." In their reports they define a typology of drug-use based on these two dimensions – conventionality and criminality. By using two scales of these dimensions they define four general categories in which a drug-user is likely to develop. These are:

1 High conventionality with low criminality – called "conformists."
2 High conventionality with high criminality – "two-worlders."
3 Low conventionality with low criminality – "the uninvolved."
4 Low conventionality with high criminality – "hustlers."

These are not four watertight compartments but a framework within which a large population can be broadly classified along the two basic dimensions which are, in fact, capable of general application. Any member of the population could be assigned a place along these two dimensions.

This study is a novel attempt to examine possible relationships between drug-use and an individual's style of life, and to explore the needs that may be served by drug-use. Such a study opens up areas for wider examination of the behaviour of drug-users and compares well with many wider studies of personality which are marred by observer bias.

In conclusion we can say that much of the work carried out on personal factors involved in drug-dependence has been concerned with a severe but narrow field of drug-dependence – that involving opiates. Many of these studies are about institutionalized patients and must be regarded with caution because of their selectivity. A conservative conclusion would be that present knowledge suggests that hospitalized opiate-addicts are people who have a history of severe personality problems prior to their taking up drugs. There are patients who use drugs to relieve psychiatric symptoms, but so far these appear to be a minority. We have scanty information about the personal factors involved in people dependent on other drugs, and it is dangerous to generalize about all drug-users on the basis of findings in hospitalized opiate users. In the field of alcoholism the personal factors involved appear to be much more diffuse and merit special consideration of their own.

Chapter 7

Drug-dependence and alcoholism: epidemiology and social factors

Any inquiry into environmental influences on aberrant behaviour is bound to be difficult, whether we are considering the misuse of drugs or alcohol, delinquency, or any socially-disturbing behaviour which presents problems to the community. Proper study is often limited by the difficulty of planning an inquiry which will avoid errors likely to render the results meaningless or misleading. The population under study has to be carefully sampled: it should be of adequate size, and properly stratified, that is genuinely representative. It must be properly matched against a control sample which is also properly stratified, and matched as closely as possible for age and sex. Reports of individual cases and their environmental characteristics are of interest – but such studies are limited by the lack of any comparison with control subjects. A properly-controlled social inquiry is likely to be protracted: it needs time, effort and financial backing. Well-directed research will frequently lead to the discovery of further questions to be answered rather than solely providing clear answers to the original questions. It is notoriously easy to make vague generalizations: the danger in speculation is that questionable inferences may be drawn from the inadequate information. Let me give an example. Someone remarked on the number of left-handed actors seen on television, in films and in the theatre, and wondered if left-handedness was more common among actors in particular than among the population, at large. Now in order to study this question adequately, one needs to know the distribution of left-handedness throughout the general population and compare this with the incidence of left-handedness in a representative sample of actors, using, say, a sample of members of Equity (the actors' trade union). But would this sample be sufficient? Should one also include actors and would-be-actors, and what about amateur actors? Also it is known that cerebral dominance, which determines right-handedness or left-handedness, may be hard to demonstrate without further testing. We may find in the end that the apparent abnormality is not really representative.

In behavioural studies biased observations can easily influence the statement of general behavioural laws but nowadays, it is hoped, any psychiatrist who based a theory of behaviour purely on his own experience of patients would have his statements closely questioned. Unhappily the questions of alcoholism and drug-dependence have received a good deal of biased theorizing. This no doubt reflects the inherent weaknesses of our methods of inquiry. It does seem that we are rather too ready in providing quick answers to serious social questions. The data obtained may be inconclusive; one worker's results may conflict with another's – this again may indicate inadequate methods of survey. The background and environmental subjects which are of interest obviously include study of the influence of age, sex, racial origin, education, work, and family structure and relationships. An attempt will be made to review a little of what is known about these subjects.

ALCOHOLISM

In Western society alcoholism is mainly found among adult males. The ratio of male to female alcoholics is around four to one. Chronic alcoholism tends to develop in the middle years of life, because, it is thought, continued use of alcohol over a long period produces a loss of control and gradually evolves particular drinking patterns. It is important to have some idea of the extent of drinking amongst the general population. A large-scale survey carried out in America in 1966 suggested that nearly 70 per cent of American adults had taken at least one alcoholic drink in the preceding year, whilst 20 per cent of the population reported that they had never taken alcohol. This background information is useful when we attempt to estimate the number of alcoholics in the population. The traditional indices used include the number of deaths resulting from alcoholism – but these may contain large margins of error.

Jellinek (1957) proposed a formula for calculating the prevalence of alcoholism in a given country. This formula was based on the number of deaths from alcoholic cirrhosis of the liver in a given year. Later he discounted the value of this formula, but it has been quite widely used by the World Health Organization, which estimated that alcoholics in the UK numbered 400,000, and in the US numbered 5 million.

It is important to consider such figures in their historical context. As far as we know, national drinking habits *do* change over the years. Accounts of drinking in eighteenth- and nineteenth-century England suggest that alcoholism and heavy drinking were more serious social problems then than they are now. But it also seems that moderation was uncommon during that period. People either indulged in heavy spirit-drinking or they abstained altogether. Nowadays drinking is both more widespread throughout the population and more moderate.

Certain races seem more at risk in the development of alcoholism. In the United Kingdom the Irish and Scots lead the field. Mental-hospital admission rates for alcoholism are four times as high in Scotland as in England. In America people of Irish and northern European stock are strongly represented in the alcoholic population but the Scots are mysteriously rare. In America the black American accounts for a very large proportion of the alcoholic population. Is this a truly ethnic association, or is it related to the low economic status of the black American?

Answer to such questions are not easily provided but happily in recent years there has been an increase of interest in the epidemiology of alcoholism.

EPIDEMIOLOGICAL STUDIES IN ALCOHOLISM

The term "epidemiology" was originally confined to the study of an infectious illness. It is now widely applied throughout medicine to the study of the incidence (new cases) and prevalence (total number of cases at a given time) of disorders in a population and their relation to causes operating within the community.

One of the basic difficulties in any study of alcoholism is primarily an epidemiological one. It is hard to determine accurately just what are the numbers of those affected. The importance of discovering the true numbers cannot be overemphasized. Failure to do so leaves us with the uncertainties of speculation. The relationship between alcoholism and social influences is self-evident, and this evidence is supported by common sense, observation and history. It is to be hoped that careful epidemiological observation of alcoholism may throw light on the pattern of development and relate its causes to social forces.

Another important difficulty in estimating the number of alcoholics arises from the fact that alcoholism is a disorder that doctors often seem unable to recognize. Besides, the patients are often reluctant to admit to themselves or to others that their problems are in any way connected with alcohol. Thus doctor and patient may unwittingly collude with each other in overlooking the real disorder.

We referred earlier to a national survey on drinking habits carried out in America. It might be considered a rational extension of this to mount a full-scale national survey aimed at discovering the true prevalence of alcoholism. Such studies unfortunately cost time and money, but it is possible to obtain information in a less cumbersome way by means of sampling. The public might well regard such national surveys as unwelcome intrusions, for many people would have misgivings about a census that included inquiries about their drinking habits. Encroachment on personal privacy and liberty *does* occur, and this is something that over-zealous researchers seem to overlook. This problem can be avoided by estimating the prevalence of alcoholism from figures provided by doctors, social-workers, the police and probation officers. An excellent example of this type of study over a three-year period was reported on by Moss and Beresford Davies (1967) who carried out a survey of the extent of alcoholism throughout Cambridgeshire. They made use of thirteen sources of information: hospital records, private psychiatric case records, general practitioners, the police, the probation service, Salvation Army hostels, Church Army hostels, children's departments, the NSPCC, marriage-guidance bureaux, Alcoholics Anonymous, the Samaritans, and the local health authority.

All the agencies contacted completed detailed questionnaires about alcoholic patients with whom they had been in touch over a three-year period. The questions related to the alcoholic himself, the effects of alcoholism on both him and his family, and any disturbance resulting to the community.

The findings indicated a rate for alcoholism of 62 per 10,000 of the male population of Cambridgeshire aged fifteen and over, and 14 per 10,000 of the female population. This result relates to a three-year period and differs from the overall figure of 110 per 10,000 of the population of England as calculated by Keller and Egron (1955). It also differs from the estimate of Parr (1957), based on general practitioners' answers to questionnaires, which gave a figure of 11 per 10,000. The authors make comment on these differences in the figures but point out that their own sources of inquiry were particularly far-reaching. At all events their inquiry was unusually carefully carried out, especially as the criticism usually levelled at this type of study is lack of detail.

General population studies would seem the most useful line of inquiry. Those already made tend to come from countries with a long tradition of keeping detailed population records. The Scandinavian countries are rightly esteemed in this respect; their records are very detailed, and have never been misused for unscrupulous ends. Also in Scandinavia the populations are generally relatively static: they do not move around much within their own countries.

One of the most interesting Scandinavian studies was that carried out by Fremming (1951) who examined the extent of psychiatric disorders on the island of Bornholm, which lies off the coast of Denmark. Bornholm, incidentally, occupies a special place in medical history, for it was here that "Bornholm disease" was first recognized and described. The population selected by Fremming consisted of 5,500 people born on the island between the years 1883 and 1887, and was followed up until 1939. The sample was truly representative of the island population for that period and the study yielded valuable data on the extent of psychiatric disorders there. As regards alcoholism, the important finding was that the expectancy rate was 3·4 per cent for men and 0·1 per cent for women.

However, it is unusual for an investigator to come across an adequately-sized sample of a relatively static population like this one, so an alternative approach is to take a well-defined area such as a city or large town and examine the drinking patterns of a sample of the population. A fairly recent example of this sort of study was that of Mulford and Miller (1960), who reported on the drinking habits of 1,185 Iowans. The inquiry was based on the subjects' own accounts of their drinking habits and showed that 9 per cent of the sample could be regarde as "heavy drinkers." This figure should not be regarded as the prevalence rate of alcoholism as such, but rather as a clue to the proportion of people in a population who run more than an average risk of developing alcoholism later on.

Another highly detailed American study was that of Bailey *et al.* (1965), who surveyed Washington Heights, a residential area in Manhattan. The sample examined was drawn at random and covered more than 4,000 families, including over 8,000 persons. One member of each family was interviewed about the consumption of alcohol in that family and to relate any behaviou which might suggest alcoholism. As was essential, the authors used well-defined criteria for identifying alcoholism, and they checked the reliability of their assessment by means of a later study. Their main finding was a total alcoholism rate of 19 per 1,000. An intriguing discovery in the later study was that a further 10 per cent were identified as alcoholic, whilst 25 per cent of the people who previously gave a history of alcoholism now denied it.

It will now be clear that it is not easy to make accurate assessments of the extent of alcoholism, even when relatively sophisticated methods of inquiry are used.

TRANSCULTURAL STUDIES

Any attempt to compare the prevalence rate of alcoholism or drug-dependence between one country and another is bound to run into difficulties unless the relative figures are examined objectively, and not exposed to any speculation. In the first place, despite the *official* definitions of alcoholism, there may be many differences in the cultural attitudes of countries towards alcohol: thus someone loosely regarded as an alcoholic in one country may not be considered so in another. Sometimes relatively simple factors can affect consumption rates: some countrie are able to produce more alcohol than others, for example through cultivation of the vine. Drinking preferences may differ widely, or relate primarily to what is locally produced: the United States and the United Kingdom prefer beer and spirits, whilst in Italy, Spain and France wine is the universal drink.

Jellinek (1962) had some interesting comments to make on

alcoholism in France and Italy. There is a considerable difference between the prevalence rates for alcoholism in France and Italy: in 1953 the World Health Organization ranked France second to America in national alcoholism rates, and Italy twelfth on the list – with the rate in France five times higher than that in Italy (2,850 per 100,000 against 500 per 100,000). He remarked that France and Italy have alcohol-producing industries of similar size, and that in each country roughly the same proportion of land is given over to wine-growing. It has been asserted in the past that the high incidence of alcoholism in France is tied up with the interests of the alcohol industry, but Jellinek's comparisons with Italy have since suggested that it is an over-simplification to relate alcoholism in France to economic pressures alone.

However Jellinek did comment on the real differences in the way the two nations consume alcohol. The French have more of a tendency to drink wine at any time of the day. Anyone who has visited northern France must be aware of this after seeing farm-labourers drinking spirits on their way to work in the morning. In Italy, however, drinking is more closely confined

Alcohol as part of the social tradition: a British stag party in which medical students rag one of their colleagues who is about to get married

to meal-times. Also a much smaller quantity of spirits is drunk in Italy, and drunkenness is viewed unfavourably there.

In France public awareness of the dangers of drinking spirits has lately been expressed (1970) in new regulations imposed by the Government which limit severely the advertising of drinks of high spirit-content of the anisette variety. These have a well-justified reputation for being dangerous intoxicants. In Poland recognition of these dangers has led to the banning of advertisements for alcohol. To a lesser degree they have also been recognized in the United Kingdom and the United States where television commercials for brands of alcohol are subjected to a moderate degree of restraint, which could well be extended.

SOME SOCIOLOGICAL VIEWS OF ALCOHOLISM

Bales (1946) put forward a general sociological theory of alcoholism, wherein the drinking practices of a culture are related to the level of its social organization. His yardstick is threefold. First of all must be assessed the extent to which a culture exerts pressures on its members sufficient to produce "minor tensions" within them. Secondly, must be considered the attitudes towards drinking which prevail among the members of the culture, and thirdly, to what extent the culture provides its people with a means of satisfaction other than alcohol.

One of his comments on cultural attitudes to alcohol was that "the crucial factor seems to be whether a given attitude towards drinking positively suggests drinking to the individual as a means of relieving his inner tensions or whether it arouses counter-anxiety." He suggested four basic cultural attitudes to drinking: the ritual, convivial, abstinent and utilitarian attitudes. An example of the abstinent attitude is found in Muslim countries, where alcohol is forbidden on religious grounds. An example of the ritual attitude is found among Jews, where alcohol is bound up with orthodox religious observance: this makes drinking a sacred act, and therefore drunkenness becomes an abomination, an act of sacrilege.

Horton (1943) made a comparative study of the use of alcohol among fifty-six primitive societies. For these, information was available about quantities of alcohol consumed, and how easily it could be obtained. There was also information about the

Some advertisements for alcohol stress its supposedly virile qualities

prevalence of "relative subsistance anxiety," which means the underlying fear of being unable to acquire and maintain the basic needs of existence. He found that a clear correlation seemed to exist between high levels of "subsistence anxiety" and heavy drinking: the higher the level of worry over crop-failure, floods, etc., the higher was the rate of drinking. He drew the general conclusion that alcohol has the "unequivocally significant" property of being able to lessen anxiety, and that this fundamentally determines the degree of its use in different societies – depending on the level of "subsistence anxiety" and ultimately on its availability.

Mowrer and Mowrer (1945) saw alcohol use in society in a different light. First they saw it as an intoxicant which helped the adult to reinstate himself into a lost but superior role which he had enjoyed in childhood; secondly they considered that alcoholism could be related directly to the degree of social change and disorganization within a community. They suggested that alcoholism was therefore likely to be more prevalent in central urban areas than in outlying areas. This may well be true, as it is true of mental illness, suicide and delinquency; but to prove a *causal* relationship is something very different, since it can be argued with equal force that it is people afflicted by severe social problems who will tend to drift more easily into the rootless and transient situations of central urban life.

We can say, then, that our understanding of social factors as causes of alcoholism is far from clear, although our expectation of their importance is high. Certainly a relationship is indicated by the fact that particular ethnic groups will have consistently high or low rates of alcohol-use in areas where availability of alcohol is constant. It is likely that our understanding of this phenomenon can only be clarified by long-term studies of both normal and abnormal drinkers.

Early childhood experience is thought to be important in influencing a person's later drinking habits. This concerns not only the relationship between parent and child but, even simpler, the possible effect of parental drinking on the child. It is commonly found that alcoholics come from alcoholic families, and also that the children of alcoholics show rates of psychiatric disturbance in childhood five times higher than control groups of children. Other studies have shown that the children of a marriage where one parent is an alcoholic have a 25 per cent risk of later developing alcoholism. The present view is that this is more likely to result from parental example than from genetic inheritance. Clearly a child's first experience of adults using alcohol may be crucial. It is generally found that where the child first sees alcohol used in the setting of a formalized ritual, as in Judaism, then he is more likely to learn control over alcohol by appreciating its special place in his culture. Where alcohol is used by the family in social rituals, meals and celebrations, or where drinking in the family is restrained and supervised, then the child has a better chance of becoming a normal drinker.

Introduction to the function of alcohol in early childhood, when witnessed on the part of responsible adults, is not necessarily a bad thing. On the other hand a highly-vulnerable group of young people are those who begin drinking in late adolescence outside the home; they are more likely to become heavy drinkers of spirits.

In many respects some of our best factual information linking early family experience with the use and abuse of alcohol has come from the study of Jewish people. It has often been observed that on the whole Jews rarely become alcoholics. The reports of Snyder (1958, 1962) on the drinking habits of Jewish students in American colleges has thrown considerable light on this, as have also the observations of Glatt (1970). It is generally found that orthodox Judaism uses alcohol in sacred situations and that the judicious constraints of religion and family influence ensure that a child learns respect for, fear of, and control over alcohol. There is also evidence that a drift away from orthodox Judaism carries with it a higher risk of alcohol problems. It is found too that Jewish people may well select other forms of intoxicants, ones which are not invested with religious significance, such as drugs.

It may be felt that such findings relating to minority groups cannot be related to the experience of the general population, but it is the author's view that these findings are of such crucial importance that they cannot be shrugged off in this way. If the fact of becoming a problem drinker with subsequent loss of control is at least partially influenced by early experiences, then this must have *some* bearing on efforts to prevent alcoholism.

The plight of the poor people in eighteenth-century England, depraved by the gin-houses, is shown in Hogarth's "Gin Lane" (1751)

OCCUPATION AND ALCOHOLISM

Surveys of alcoholics indicate that some occupations do carry a high risk of alcoholism. These include employment in the liquor trade and occupations where alcohol is used for business entertainment. Possibly a kind of selection may operate in that people who have beginnings of an alcohol problem may consciously or unconsciously choose such jobs. There are some occupations which encourage easy relief from a high level of tension by the ready availability of alcohol for entertainment purposes.

ALCOHOLISM, SOCIAL CLASS AND ITS RELATION TO POVERTY

In the eighteenth and nineteenth centuries when heavy spirit-drinking was cheap and common in the United Kingdom, alcohol was widely abused by those who led lives of hopelessness in the

The distilling of illicit poteen in Ulster prior to the First World War

face of severe poverty. Nowadays the relationship between alcoh and poverty is less distinct. For a start, spirit-drinking is now expensive. The differing rates of alcoholism between one social class and another are hard to evaluate. In general in this country the highest admission rates for alcoholic psychosis and alcoholism are reported in social class I, with an excess of deaths from alcoholic cirrhosis also in social class I.

American reports, however, while confirming high rates in upper social classes, continue to show high rates among people of low socio-economic status. The general impression derived in Western countries is that alcoholism is rarest in middle social groups, so that alcoholism affects the highly-affluent and the poorest groups but not in the middle. It is interesting to note a tendency for upper-class and middle-class alcoholics to be described as "problem drinkers" or to be labelled under polite psychiatric terms, whilst the same condition among lower-class people is more likely to be described as "chronic drunkenness." So once again class bias on the part of the observer may be at wo here. An eventual fall-off in work and earning power is the rule in the progress of alcoholism, and this is a consequence of the lowered efficiency.

MARITAL STATUS

The bulk of studies show a high incidence of unmarried people among alcoholic populations. This will result from the break-up of marriages caused by alcoholism, though there is also a significant proportion of people who have never married. Widowers, too, appear to be at risk: loss of control over their drinking may occur after the wife's death.

ALCOHOL AND SUICIDE

Numerous reports reiterate the high rate of association between alcoholism and suicide, and attempted suicide. American reports show that hospital admissions for attempted suicide rate alcoholi as high as 30 per cent. A study in Scotland (Batchelor 1954) involving 200 consecutive admissions for attempted suicide showed that 21 per cent of the subjects had a clear history of excessive drinking. Reports such as those of Ringel and Rotter (1957) from Vienna showed that 15 per cent of a one-year sampl of suicide attempts concerned people who were drunk at the time, and that half of these were chronic alcoholics. In Finland, Saarenheimo (1952) found that 25 per cent of post-mortems on suicides revealed that they had killed themselves under the influence of alcohol.

It is generally agreed that an alcoholic is more likely to kill himself than is a non-alcoholic. One receives the overall impression that the alcoholic who kills himself is likely to be older and living in a socially-isolated state, usually with a past history of suicide attempts and depression. These findings have been supported by those of Kessel (1965) in this country: he clearly defined the links between alcohol and suicide.

ALCOHOL AND CRIME

In general we can say that there are definite links between alcohol and crime but it is hard to delineate them clearly. An obvious area of inquiry involves alcohol and murder. Probably the most extensive study in this connection was carried out by Wolfgang (1968), who found from a study of nearly 600 murder cases in Philadelphia that in only 36 per cent of the cases could alcohol be ruled out in both victim and accused, whilst in 44 per cent of the cases alcohol was present in both victim and accused.

As regards theft, alcohol seems to be associated only with rather crude attempts; but concerning other criminal behaviour the suggestion is that alcohol can act to lower a person's control over impulses that he normally keeps in order; and this can lead to criminal activity, as in certain sexual offences. The same is probably true of alcoholism in relation to violence in general.

The "professional," skilled and competent criminal generally does not act under the influence of alcohol, since its effect on his judgement is soon recognized. Indeed, the drinking criminal is usually held in low regard by his more competent and abstaining associates.

ALCOHOL AND ROAD TRAFFIC ACCIDENTS

Since alcohol impairs sensation, perception, performance, judgement and co-ordination, it is not surprising that it plays a considerable part in road accidents. In fact the studies carried out are relatively consistent in showing a clear relationship between drinking and accidents. The percentages for incidents where alcohol is a factor in accidents varies from country to country (Andreasson, 1962), for example:

Spain	1·5 per cent
Belgium	2·0 per cent
Sweden	2·9 per cent
Finland	7·6 per cent

Plymar (1955) reported that in 25·4 per cent of fatal accidents in California in 1951, either a pedestrian or a driver had been drinking.

Other reports have noted that alcohol is implicated in 50 per cent of accidents occurring after 10 p.m. Perhaps the most consistent findings is that blood alcohol-levels correlate highly with the extent of damage and injury. The "drink-and-drive" driver involved in accidents is, in America at least, likely to be someone with a very high blood alcohol-level, since studies there do not confirm the popular idea that such drivers are just casual social drinkers who have been unlucky. American studies suggest there possibly exists an important group of accident-prone drivers with very high blood alcohol-levels. This means the drinking driver is more likely to have an accident than is the non-drinker, and drinking drivers are involved in a high percentage of all accidents. It should be clear from these straightforward findings that the relationship between alcohol and road accidents reveals one of the most clearly defined causes for dangerous behaviour. Opinion which argues against the use of the breathalyser, or indeed of any other reasonable measure to try and reduce road deaths, has really no case. Even the most minute quantity of alcohol may impair driving performance.

DRUG-DEPENDENCE – ENVIRONMENTAL FACTORS

There is a good deal of information available about the type of background common to drug-users in the United States, and a growing pool of information about those in the United Kingdom but despite the relative profusion of American data or the relative paucity of English data, in fact much of it is inconclusive, and some of it is even misleading and possibly irrelevant. But then, serious study of drug-dependence is comparatively new: even in recent times the subject was one that tended to discourage researchers. In America there have been legal and other reasons for this, and in the United Kingdom it is due to the relative rarity of dependence and thus the lack of urgency. Data in this country is accumulating, but is as yet inconclusive. Much of it has been collected during a period when the problem has been increasing rapidly, so the data gives us only cross-sections of the situation rather than a long-term picture.

A review of some important findings in the United States should not be out of place here, though one cannot assume that findings in this country will be similar. It is always dangerous to try and transpose the significance of findings from one culture to another. On the face of it, the situation of a black slum-dwelling drug-user from New York City is likely to be very different from that of a young lower-middle-class English drug-user from a London suburb. For while in either case one may acknowledge that the personality problems of the two youngsters might be very similar, clearly their environments are very different.

Much of the background information (the demography) of American drug-users as known to official agencies has been concisely reviewed by Winick (1965), and the main contents of his review will be described here. His report, in this case, was an attempt to give an overall view of the epidemiology of narcotic-drug-abuse in America, and interestingly enough, it begins with a reference to the fact that although United States law-enforcement agencies had the bulk of contact with drug-users over the years, there was nevertheless a remarkable shortage of available information. The report considers first the basic question of numbers. The main systematic records on the numbers of opiate-users in the United States are those kept by the Federal Bureau of Narcotics. It presents annual reports numbering the violations of the drug laws and the numbers of drug-users who have come to the Bureau's attention during a given year. Once an addict's name is in the Bureau's files it remains on the "active" list for five years. If there are no further reports it goes onto the "inactive" list for another five years and no longer appears in the Bureau's annual returns.

Winick and others (Chein 1964) have pointed out a basic flaw in FBN reporting in that no indication is given of the *extent* of drug-use within this period by individuals named on the files, so that while the figures refer to numbers of "addicts," there are good grounds for suspecting that some of these addicts may have become "inactive" well before the five-year period has elapsed. A considerable climate of criticism surrounds the FBN records: one recurrent theme is that the FBN may have far fewer people reported to them than actually do exist, since the agencies which would otherwise notify them may fear that drug-users would then be arrested. Nevertheless the FBN figures are the *only* national figures available from America and do give a fair indication of general trends there. For example, in 1931 the Bureau reported 4,534 people as violaters of Federal narcotic laws, but by 1958 the national total was 46,266. By 1962 the total was 47,489. It is interesting to note that as many as 10,882 *new* cases were reported in 1955.

Now, such numbers are difficult to interpret: it was said that at the turn of the century there were one million opiate-addicts in America; yet by the end of the 1914–18 war this number had mysteriously shrunk to 250,000. It may be assumed that these early reports were badly founded, and that official United States figures from the late 1920s onwards are a relatively accura account of the extent of the problem. But these official figures cannot give the number of people in the community who are using drugs but have not been discovered by official agencies – the police, FBN or treatment agencies.

Discussing these figures, Winick (1965) remarked that by then there appeared to be a relative constancy in the numbers of new drug-users reported annually, suggesting that the incidence of drug-use in America "has reached a certain stability, with a fairly constant number entering the new user population each year and a fairly stable proportion becoming inactive."

This was an interesting and challenging statement from an authority whose knowledge of the epidemiology of drug-use in the United States is unquestioned. Yet in the years following 1965 there were many who denied a relative constancy of the numbers of addicts, remarking that daily experience suggested the growth rate of heroin-addiction in urban USA was reaching epidemic proportions. Numbers as high as 100,000 for heroin-addicts in New York were quoted, in the various media, often with histrionic clarity, although no factual evidence was offered in support. Certainly by 1968 and 1969 many reliable authorities in New York were suggesting that 40,000 would be a feasible estimate for the heroin-addicts in the city. The wide divergence in such estimates deserves examination, for the trends are germane to the situation in the United Kingdom.

First of all what is the significance of a total of 40,000 addicts? Does it comprise regular daily users who are all physically dependent. This is hard to accept considering the heavily adulterated state of the heroin obtainable: so adulterated is it that in hospital experience, moderate or severe physical dependence is uncommon, and, besides, so many drug-users could not all support the expense involved. But if it were true that the 40,000 were all markedly physically dependent, then the figure would indeed be alarming. If, however, the figure of 40,000 includes irregular users and those with little or no physical dependence, then, though still serious, it must be viewed in a different light.

So, whatever the discontent with official FBN figures, such alternative estimates are less than likely to indicate the real number of those who are truly dependent. However, a middle-of-the-road view would consider them less far out than their more severe critics maintain.

AGE

In America the fall in age-level of those using drugs for the first time is clearly documented. Of 1,660 violators of narcotics laws in 1929, 47 per cent were under twenty-four, and 19 per cent were between twenty-five and twenty-nine. Of 1,036 admissions to the USPHS hospital in Lexington in 1936–7, 44 per cent were under twenty-four, 25·1 per cent were between twenty-five and twenty-nine, and 14·2 per cent were between thirty and thirty-four.

In the years following the Second World War the age-level of those starting on drugs dropped strikingly. Thus, though Zimmering was unable to discover one adolescent drug-user in the records of Belle Vue Hospital, New York, between 1940 and 1948, he found six in 1950, and eighty-four in the first two months of 1951. And this trend was reflected in Federal records.

When considering this drop in age of first drug-use it is noted that there are always relatively few older drug-users in official records. Winick has examined this to find a reason. It is known that some drug-users die off from overdose, infection and violent death (homicide, suicide and accident), and others die of neglect and malnutrition: possibly such deaths are not fully reported. But Winick points out that the low representation of older addicts may well suggest a natural process of "maturing-out" of opiate-addiction. He believes the *majority* of users may leave off drugs in their thirties because at that age they no longer receive their earlier satisfaction, and by then maturation in age is drawing the user towards more realistic life goals – employment, marriage and starting a family. By the time he reaches his thirties a person is less susceptible to aggressive and sexual drives, and is more likely to have learnt something from corrective experiences such as probation and imprisonment.

This theory of "maturing out" has been criticized on the basis that it sees drug-usage as a haphazard process and would thus encourage a laissez-faire attitude to drug-users: if he has a good chance of maturing out eventually, why bother with him now?

But this is far removed from what Winick is really getting at. His comments on maturing out are derived from careful mathematical analysis of the age drop-off curves, and are backed up by findings in other, related fields. First of all there is delinquency. Most of the data clearly suggests that delinquency reaches its peak in early and mid teens, and gradually falls away to disappear in the thirties and forties – so in a sense it can be regarded as a self-limiting condition. Furthermore there is a good body of evidence to suggest that many aggressive and unstable psychopaths tend to shed their more antisocial behaviour with the passage of time. It would be surprising perhaps if a complicated and relatively antisocial type of behaviour such as drug-dependence, having recognized links with criminality, did not also show a fall-off with increasing age and psychological maturity.

In the United States it is calculated that the mean duration of drug-use of the "average" drug-user is around nine years. It is said that the "average" user is likely to run foul of the law in around two years from his first drug-use. On the other hand, in a study of English and New York case records, Willis (1971) particularly noted that a number of users in America had managed to maintain regular drug-use for up to fifteen years before any contact with treatment or with law-enforcement agencies. Such evidence suggests that drug-users can survive in the community relatively successfully, and that their ability to do so may be seriously underestimated.

SEX

For drug-dependence the ratio of men to women is found to be five to one. Leading up to this, there appears to have been a marked change in this ratio over the last eighty years in America. In 1929, out of 1,660 new drug-users there, 1,317 were men and 276 were women; in Chicago in the early 1930s, 73 per cent were men and 27 per cent were women. The Federal Bureau of Narcotics reported in 1955 that 77 per cent of its recorded users were men and 23 per cent were women. At the end of 1962 it reported 38,654 men and 8,835 women – a ratio therefore of about five to one.

However, going back in time one finds statements that before the turn of the century something like 80 per cent of opiate-users in the United States were women. Indeed at the time the opiate drugs seem to have been a medication traditionally favoured by women, who took them for all varieties of pain. Perhaps this high proportion of women quoted may have resulted from them becoming dependent on opiates through using them for therapeutic purposes. No doubt, with the passage of time women shifted to the use of more socially-acceptable pain-relieving drugs.

ETHNICITY

In America considerable information is available about the racial and national origin of drug-users. For instance, in the Belle Vue Hospital in New York in the late 1920s, out of 318 voluntary admissions for the treatment of drug-dependence, 310 were white and eight were Negro. In 1935 a sample of Californian drug-users revealed 59 per cent white, 40 per cent Negro, and 16 per cent oriental. But after the Second World War an increasing proportion of non-white users was recorded so that by 1962 the FBN reported 54·9 per cent to be Negro, 10·9 per cent Puerto Rican (white), 7·2 per cent Mexican (white), and 25·9 per cent other whites.

There is no doubt that since the Second World War, particularly in large cities like New York, there has been an explosion of heroin-use amongst under-privileged racial-minority groups living in areas of extreme socio-economic deprivation. It may well be that this notion that under-privileged coloured and Puerto Rican drug-users represent the bulk of the addict population has given rise to a number of false preconceptions and assumptions about the epidemiology of drug-use in contemporary America.

THE PHYSICAL ENVIRONMENT

Much of the information available from America relates drug-use to town-dwellers highly concentrated in slum areas. This seems to have been accepted as an article of faith until about 1968. Since then the emergence of the relatively affluent middle-class white drug-user suggests that drug-use has spread to a wider section of the population. Nevertheless, there is a good backlog of data which defines poor socio-economic status as a crucial contributor to increase in the use of opiates in America.

In the 1920s the majority of drug-users examined were found to have poorly defined occupations with a history of irregular employment; and the same was true of the 1930s when in Chicago 78·6 per cent of a sample examined were people whose economic status was said to be "marginal." Against this one needs to consider the fact that better-off drug-users can usually get by in society and will not be revealed to official agencies.

These official findings were reiterated in data obtained since the end of the Second World War. Whatever may be the survival capacity of middle-class Americans, one cannot ignore the real links of opiate-dependence with poverty, lack of expectations, and the realization of lack of simple opportunity for self-betterment – and this in a society that places a prime value on self-betterment but rejects state aid for the underprivileged in terms such as "creeping socialism" and "socialized medicine."

SOCIAL AND ECONOMIC ASPECTS OF HEROIN-USAGE IN NEW YORK

A recent study of the social and economic aspects of heroin-usage has been provided by Preble, a professor of anthropology, and Casey, an academic economist, in a report (1969) entitled "Taking care of business: the heroin-user's life on the streets."

Under-privileged heroin-addicts (Scene in Hong Kong in 1959)

The authors describe the life-styles and general social activity of heroin-users from slum areas in New York, who, at the time of publication at least, probably represented 80 per cent of the heroin-using population of New York.

In commenting on the general proposition that heroin-users employ the drug as a means of escape from personal problems and extreme environmental difficulties, the authors refer to the many relevant studies in this field, including those of Chein *et al.* (1964) and Cloward and Ohlin (1960). These studies represent the user as typically a person of passive, dependent, rather inadequate personality make-up who has retreated from society into drug-use as a means of insulating himself from frustration, from having to make decisions, and from the general business of living. But Preble and Casey question the validity of such observations and present an interesting and provocative anthropological and economic analysis of their findings. Their contention is that the drug-using of slum-dwelling heroin-addicts is "anything but an escape from life." They see drug-use as a highly-organized system of productive, though basically antisocial behaviour in which the transient satisfactions of drug-taking are only a minimal aspect of the way of life. They point out, for instance, that a sure way of identifying a user in a slum area is to observe his walk, usually "fast and purposeful," not stumbling and ill-directed. This is seen as a reflection of his being always on the move, avoiding law-enforcement officers, looking for drugs, stealing, disposing of stolen goods, etc. These activities are summed up in the heroin-user's slang phrase "taking care of business."

Their study was carried out in lower-class areas, in the Lower East Side, Harlem, Yorkville and the Bronx. Findings were based not only on participant observation and interview but on extensive field-work through which the authors came to know in great depth the whole scope of drug-usage as a career (Preble, personal communication, 1969). Reviewing the history of heroin-use in New York, they point out that between the wars it was mainly confined to the entertainment business, to professional criminals and their fringe associates. During the Second World War there was little heroin-use. In the immediate post-war period, an increased Negro and Puerto Rican immigrant population came to the city looking for work. They tended to occupy the lowest place in the social pecking order, with an expanding unemployment and delinquency rate. Amongst these people heroin became inherent to drug-using sub-cultural groups of a cohesive nature. Heroin was cheap, and economic pressures on the user were lessened as work became easier to find.

In the early 1950s the picture changed when youngsters began to use heroin, particularly street-gang fighters looking for new forms of illicit satisfactions. This kind of drug-use was followed by further illicit activity. Subsequently, in the late 1950s, another change occurred, as the large criminal syndicates began to move away from drug-trafficking, under pressure of tighter Federal law enforcement.

From 1961 onwards critical shortages of heroin occurred, known as "panics," and as the authors point out, these were the major influence on the later course of events. To extend supplies, illicitly-imported heroin was more and more heavily adulterated. Sub-cultures of drug-users began to break up, since getting the drug was so difficult and expensive that it was "every man for himself" in order to survive. Former associates became vigorous rivals and enemies. Heroin-distribution began to be organized as a clearly-defined chain of supply and profit. At the top of the hierarchy was the major importer (said to have a 300 per cent profit margin) and at the lowest end was the street seller (with a profit of 56 per cent). The extent of adulteration is hard to calculate, but has led to the present situation where heroin available at street-level is highly adulterated. A bag bought for five or six dollars may contain less than 10 mg of the drug. Physicians observed only mild withdrawal symptoms from the use of it in hospital: this is in line with the experience of the present author (Willis, 1969).

Preble and Casey made some interesting observations on the relationship between the altered availability of heroin, and the crime rate. The original stereotype user was a passive person with little potential for violence or assault, but recent findings in New York contradict this. Without presenting the evidence in detail the general influence now to be drawn is that while the user may avoid violent crimes which do not involve gain, nevertheless if gain, through robbery, is involved then users tend more to violence than non-users. The authors point out from their findings that one cannot conclude that drug-use provides an escape from life, but rather that it gives some people the means of achieving their own kind of life-style, even though this is socially unacceptable and a drain on the public economy and health services. The effort the user puts into this life-style is greatly out of proportion to the low rewards given by the drug itself. In the authors' words, "If they can be said to be addicted, it is not so much to heroin as to the entire career of a heroin-user." Their use of drugs is seen primarily as an attempt to make something meaningful out of a life with few advantages which they cannot understand in any other terms. This study presents an important challenge to many commonly-accepted notions about the lives of drug-users. The social and economic evidence presented by Preble and Casey cannot conveniently be ignored.

One may speculate about the ultimate socio-economic basis for alcohol-abuse among slum-dwellers in Britain in the nineteenth century. Extreme physical hardship and deprivation must have provided strong need for relief through intoxication, but there is no direct evidence that heavy drinkers used alcohol in a career-type function. Nevertheless social and economic factors were important determinants, as is reiterated in many other areas of drug and alcohol abuse.

Another observation on the theme of drug-addiction as a chosen antisocial career was presented by Rubington (1967) in an article entitled "Drug-addiction as a deviant career." The author noted that the term "career" derives from society's need to identify and categorize the work roles of its members. Those roles which entail prolonged training, ceremony, and high social status tend to be called professions; whilst roles entailing shorter and less complex training, little use of ceremonial, and lower social status tend to be called occupations and jobs. His main point is that these definitions provide society with useful means of classifying and approving socially acceptable ways of working regularly and being a worthy member of society. The author contrasts this behaviour with "social deviance," a term which implies the community's rejection of people whose way of life offends against public morals and expectations. Rubington makes the interesting proposition that however deviant the addict's life may be by normal standards, he still has a need to establish his social identity. He therefore follows a predictable sequence of behaviour which will proclaim his role as an addict to society and himself. In the author's words, "In so far as he does all that, he follows a career – albeit a deviant one rather than a legitimate one."

He points out that the process of becoming an addict involves a sequence of characteristic steps by which he can be identified. These include loss of control over intake of the substance, self-injury and injury to others, increased tolerance to drugs, and increased physical and psychological dependence. This is contrasted with certain social interpretations of drug-dependence – that someone may be an addict because he happens to use a drug that is illegal. The author then makes a concise and pithy refutation of much of the mythology that surrounds drug-use. For example he points out that physical damage arising from drug-use *per se* is rare, as opposed to the secondary effects of unsterile self-injection, self-neglect, and so on.

Next Rubington disposes of the contention that drugs destroy the sense of morality. He feels that drugs do not affect morality, or at least that moral judgements about drugs are likely to be invalid, since such judgements reflect an evaluation of lower-class people made by middle-class people in terms of middle-class expectations. The charge that "addicts are sexual menaces" is disposed of by citing the fact that pretty nearly all drugs are in fact sexual depressants.

Perhaps the most cogent observation made by Rubington deals with the idea that addiction is a contagious disease spread among the "uninfected" by "non-infected" drug- peddlers. He comments: "If addiction is contagious . . . it is most correctly regarded as something that is *learned* in association with other people."

Drug-using people develop their own self-images, skills norms and ideology: no doubt these are basically antisocial but they do provide the matrix of a life-style which, though deviant, brings a limited form of self-fulfilment for the drug-user. Rubington also comments that this identification with a deviant career is self-perpetuating: the addict continues to see himself in this antisocial role. And his own self-image is reinforced by the attitude of society towards him, which thus encourages him to continue this way.

CONCLUSION

Examination of carefully-obtained data suggests that opiate-usage, particularly of heroin, in America is primarily found among young males, who start drug-use for a variety of reasons: to get "high," to win peer-group acceptance, to insulate the self against the overwhelming sense of failure in a highly competitive society – often in situations of grotesque material and family deprivation, and mainly in town slum areas. Membership of low-status racial-minority groups is significant, as is membership of local sub-cultures in which a basically cynical, pessimistic and delinquent outlook on the world prevails. Recent evidence suggests, however, that drug-usage is spreading among middle-class youngsters of relative affluence, often to a surprising degree. This trend extends to areas of superlative physical comfort usually associated with high executive status. Drugs, like alcohol, have no awareness of man-made social distinctions.

THE UNITED KINGDOM

In England things happen more quietly, and so, up till the end of the Second World War narcotic drug-usage in this country

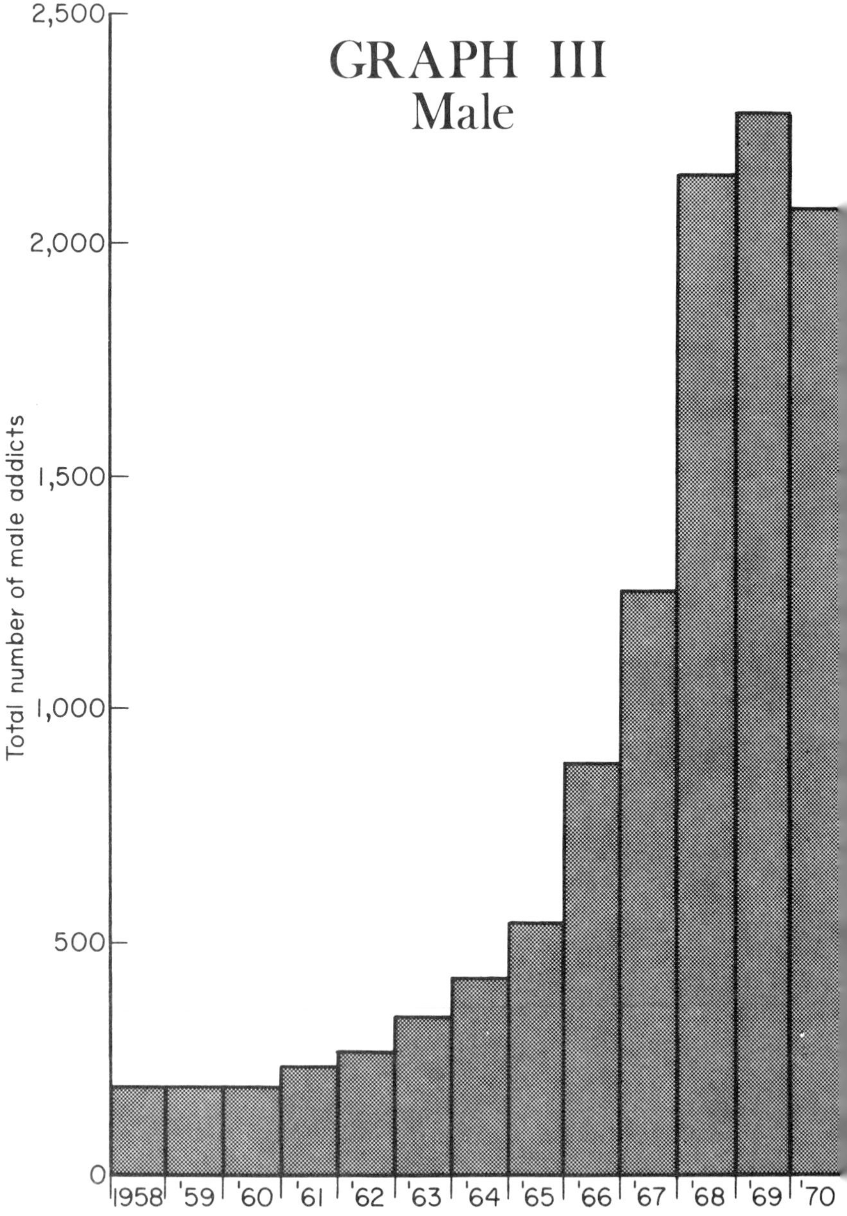
GRAPH III
Male
Total number of male addicts
2,500
2,000
1,500
1,000
500
0
1958
'59
'60
'61
'62
'63
'64
'65
'66
'67
'68
'69
'70

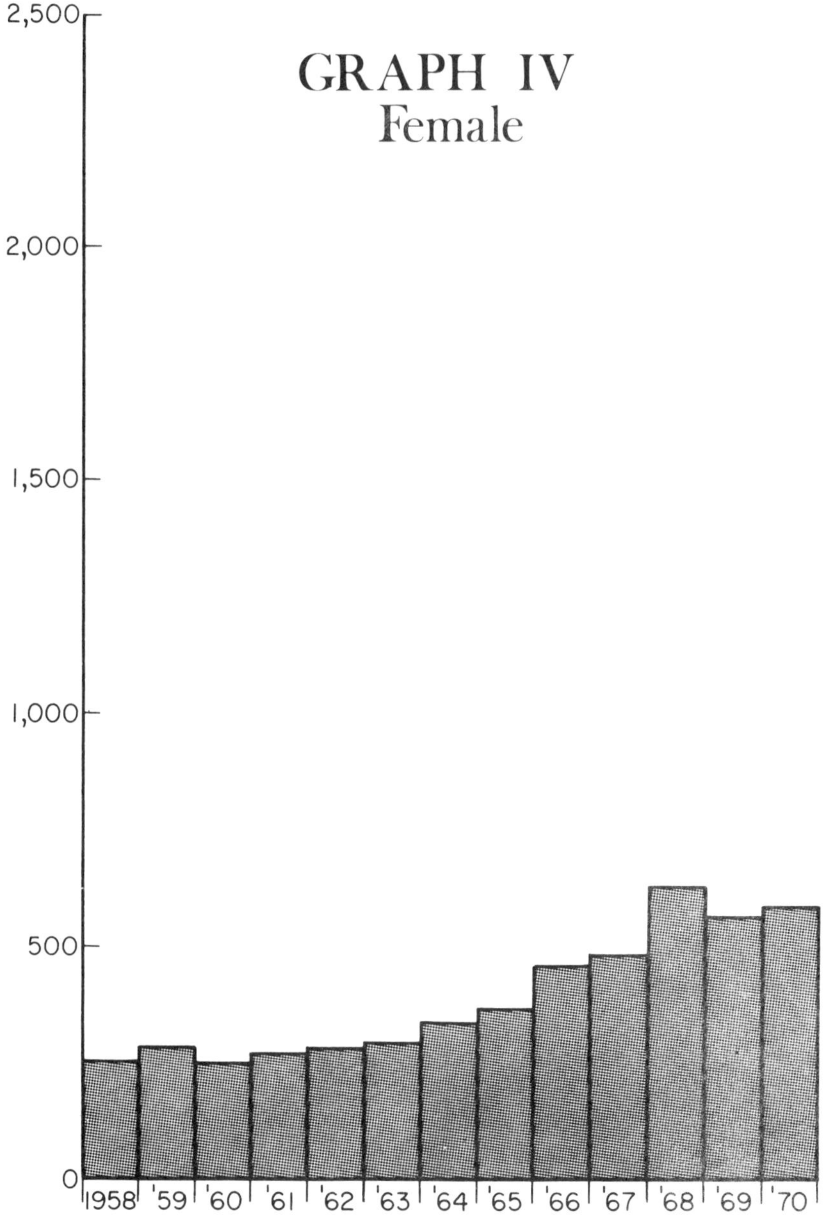

2,500
GRAPH IV
Female
2,000
1,500
1,000
500
0
1958
'59
'60
'61
'62
'63
'64
'65
'66
'67
'68
'69
'70

was confined to middle-aged people using morphine for therapeutic reasons (80 per cent), to doctors and nurses (15 per cent), and to a handful of eccentrics and exhibitionists (5 per cent). Since the increase in drug-usage, dating from the 1950s, there have been a number of reports which attempt to describe the demography of drug-usage amongst hospitalized and imprisoned drug-users (Bewley, 1969; Hewetson and Ollendorf, 1967; Gillespie *et al.*, 1967).

It is striking that an American author, Schur (1962), reporting on English drug-users, tended to confirm earlier speculations about English usage. Schur examined the job records, social class, age, sex, marital details, drug-use history, work adjustment, delinquency, etc., of drug-users in England at the time and remarked on the high proportion of medical and para-medical workers concerned. He also remarked on the relatively high social status of addicts examined, and the fact that addicts tended to be aged thirty and over. Unfortunately the study was carried out and reported on in a time of rapid change for the epidemiology of drug-use in England, so it failed to demonstrate this change, though with hindsight it is clear that the elements of the change were present at that time.

As far as the present is concerned in the United Kingdom, Schur's findings are now quite irrelevant, despite the care and intuition applied to the study. This is a good illustration of the real difficulty of trying to report on current drug-usage at any stage.

The studies of Hewetson and Ollendorf (1967), Gillespie *et al.* (1967), Bewley (1969), Willis (1969), and James (1969) suggest that drug-usage is widely spread throughout the range of social classes in the United Kingdom. They also draw attention to tantalizing links between drug-use and criminality.

The numbers of users of dangerous drugs known to the Home Office between the years 1958 and 1969 are recorded in graph 2 on page 63. In sex distribution the ratio of men to women is about five to one. Figures for 1958 - 69 are given in graphs 3 and 4. A definite lowering of age-range is discernible among those using drugs for the first time: the first recorded heroin-addict under the age of twenty was found in 1960. The following years revealed a striking change, as can be seen by referring to graph 1 on page 60.

The findings of Bewley (1969) and Willis (1969) also pointed to a fall in social class from parent to the son or daughter who was a drug-user, as measured by the occupation of the father and the drug-user. The majority of subjects they described were unmarried, and Willis (1969) further noted the incidence of parental loss through separation or divorce. He also commented on the greater incidence of psychiatric disorders, alcoholism and criminality among the parents of addicts as compared with parents of control subjects. The pathology of the addicts' parents resembled very clearly that found in non-addicted psychiatric patients (Willis 1969).

Perhaps the main points about the backgrounds of known drug (opiate)-users in the United Kingdom to date may be summed up as follows. Firstly, they tend to be young adult males whose first encounter with drugs was likely to have been prompted by pleasure-seeking reasons. Secondly at least 50 per cent of them tend to show a history of arrest and appearance in court for offences unrelated to drug-usage and prior to regular drug-taking. Thirdly, about 70 per cent have used other drugs, including amphetamines and cannabis, before taking heroin. Their family backgrounds tend to be notable for a higher than usual incidence of parental psychiatric disorder, criminality and alcoholism, and also of parental loss. The figures available to date do not suggest that these drug-users come from families markedly different from those of other delinquent youngsters, or, for that matter, different from the families of non-addicted youngsters in psychiatric hospitals.

In general the studies of addiction show that poor work-records are universal. This is not surprising, for it is not easy when young to take to drugs and work properly, though this may become easier when older. However, the drug-users so far examined tended to have poor work-records before they even started on drugs.

Although age and sex incidence may be similar to that in the United States, there is little evidence to suggest that drug-use in the United Kingdom can be primarily attributed to extreme degrees of material deprivation, as it is in America. For we have not seen extensive drug-use among youngsters here who grow up in slum areas with few hopes and prospects – youngsters who, on the American pattern, might be expected to resort to drug-use in a climate of social despair. So one has to be cautious over idle speculation about the sort of environmental influences which might lead to drug-use and -dependence. After all, even in appalling slum areas in urban USA not all of the youthful population gets involved with drugs, although a sizeable proportion will experiment with them. In families where drug-users are found the brothers and sisters are somehow able to avoid regular use of drugs, though exposed to the same family and environmental influences as the drug-users themselves. Further, they can manage to steer away from drug-use as a definite matter of choice. It seems mistaken to consider that social deprivation and poor family relationships have the power *inevitably* to drive youngsters to drugs. Such supposition leads to social theorizing about predestination. Clearly social forces and family background do make some contribution to the causes of drug-usage but it is beyond the capacity of anyone to define precisely what this contribution is and to what extent it operates.

Terms such as "social forces" and "family influences" are, unhappily, often vaguely used as a way of lending a tone of authority to mere speculation – encouraging people to speak with false certainty. The most one can say is that drug-use *may* appeal to the vulnerable and the deprived, especially those who do not have parents able to support them or capable of being real figures with whom to identify.

The psychological handicap these children have is rather difficult to define. We can do little more than generalize about it whilst realizing as humane people that their situation is a bad start for a youngster. We can go little further – to do so would be presumptuous.

Chapter 8

Drugs and delinquency

GENERAL INTRODUCTION

It is difficult to be precise in explaining the relationship which exists between drug-use and criminal behaviour. This is an area of debate where feelings tend to run high and where it seems at times almost impossible to get at the truth.

In general society shows little tolerance for drug-taking, so there is a tendency for people – both professional and lay –to make value judgements about drug-takers. They are likely to be regarded unfavourably by society – even if the unfavourable view is sugared by the word "sick" – and they may easily be held responsible for criminal acts supposedly triggered off or caused by drug-use. There is a popular belief that drugs cause people to behave violently, to commit sexual excesses, and to allow their moral standards to deteriorate. Such beliefs may be reinforced by radio, television and the press, and by incautious pronouncements by public figures like doctors, the clergy, judges and the police. As there is often very little accurate data available on which to base statements one way or the other, it is hardly surprising that it is the more dramatic comments that are the most likely to catch attention and stimulate public anxiety.

For instance it has often been asserted by writers, including the present author (Willis, 1969) that amphetamines *cause* people to behave in an aggressive and antisocial way. In fact there is very little concrete evidence to back up this statement. Reports such as those of Scott and Wilcox (1965) showed that when matched groups of amphetamine-using delinquents were compared with non-using delinquents there was no significant difference in delinquency rates. In the same vein it has been asserted that stimulant-type drugs cause road traffic accidents, but again there has been little evidence to support this. (In the case of alcohol, however, the position is clear: figures collected from all over the world indicate that alcohol is involved in roughly 50 per cent of road accidents.)

DELINQUENCY AND DRUG-USE

The relationship of delinquent behaviour to drug-use is an intrica one, and is an area that is frequently the subject of comment and conflict. So, before going into the particular issues involved in the association between crime and drugs, it is important to try and set down some of the factors that are known about delinquent behaviour in general.

A crime is regarded as taking place "when a society with recog nized ways of behaving or when a part of society which has power and authority to do so categorizes certain varieties of extreme or damaging behaviour as being liable to punishment." In considering the incidence of crime in any country one relies or the criminal statistics provided by official agencies. In England offences are divided broadly into two groups, those which are indictable and those which are not. Non-indictable offences are common and include such behaviour as drunkenness, the taking and driving away of motor vehicles, dangerous driving and certain sexual offences. In the United Kingdom approximately 60 per cent of the total number of offences dealt with by the courts are motoring offences. Yet public attention is constantly directed towards the increase in delinquent behaviour amongst the young. Delinquent behaviour has to be seen against the general social background of the United Kingdom. This is mainly a single-culture nation with a more or less stratified society. There is little organized crime and the historical and economic climate is one of gradual social development influenced by moderate radicalism. The welfare state has produced a new range of opportunity for self-betterment and on the whole a modestly acceptable degree of equality of educational opportunity

There has been a steady increase in juvenile offences in the last five or ten years. There was a sharp rise after the war up until 1951, little change between the years 1951 and 1957, and then a renewed increase. The main recent rise in juvenile delinquency occurred in the sixteen to twenty-one age-group but as pointed out by West (1967), the peak age of conviction is fourteen. Fifty per cent of the people found guilty of indictable offences lie between the ages of ten and twenty-one, but by the age of twenty-five the number convicted is half that of people aged fourteen. As in most developed countries, the main problems of delinquent behaviour concern young boys. The factors contributing to delinquent behaviour appear to be numerous, and the evidence for their importance is profuse and, at times, conflicting. For instance between the years 1935 - 6 and the years 1941-2 the sharp rise in conviction rates amongst the young produced the comment that at that time the authorities were dealing with a "delinquent generation."

It is wise, too, to be cautious about accepting figures provided by official agencies. For instance the recorded increases in offences may be affected by a number of factors. There may be changes in reporting patterns used by the police, or the public may be more ready to report certain offences, particularly those involving violence. Also victims of assault tend nowadays to report the offence rather more readily than they used to.

Another fact is that there is a clear sex difference in delinquent behaviour. In general the ratio of male to female offenders is in

A young addict spends the night in a London doorway

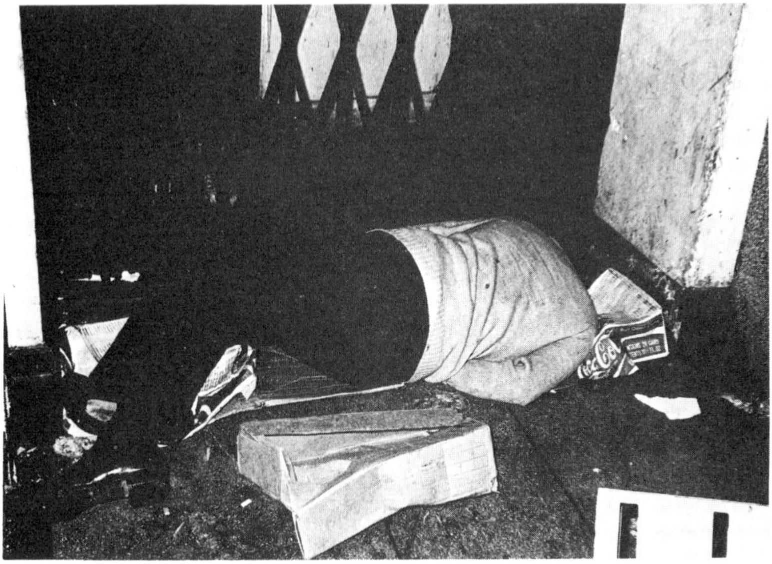

the order of six to one, but this ratio decreases with age. Many investigations have been carried out which suggest that girls and women in general have rather more conformist views on ethical and moral behaviour, and of course there are many offences which lie beyond their physical capabilities. In England, at any rate, the main offences involving women are shop-lifting, prostitution, abortion, and assaults against other women and children. Also any crimes committed by women may well be such as occur within the context of a special relationship, and so never get reported at all; for instance, the prostitute's client who has his money stolen would normally be reluctant to report her.

In general the main offences committed by the juvenile male offender in the United Kingdom are minor larcenies, taking and driving away, damage to property and also absconding. Juvenile offences tend to be most common in larger cities, and many social-workers have been able to put together a broad picture of the typical young juvenile offender. Great stress has been laid on the frequency with which these youngsters come from "broken homes." In this context it appears that divorce or separation of the parents is of greater significance than the loss of one parent by death. There is no apparent correlation between delinquency rates and intelligence as such, but the youngsters studied constantly show evidence of low educational attainment. This may well be because they are more likely to come from a domestic background where expectations are low and little interest is taken in their future prospects. Perhaps the one factor that emerges clearly is that juvenile delinquency is disproportionately high in slum areas, and that there is a very real correlation between delinquency and both poverty in the material sense and poverty of expectation in a more subtle sense.

In America investigation of the juvenile offender tends to concentrate on ethnic factors. It has been found, for instance, that disproportionate numbers of offenders are Negro slum-dwellers. However, the delinquency rates amongst blacks and whites tend to level out when black populations move into areas where they enjoy better conditions of living. An overall consideration of the juvenile offender in slum areas in the United States reveals that these youngsters may live in physical environments which are extremely bad. They are brought up in the expectation of failure in a climate of extreme disorganization in family life. Loss of one parent through separation or divorce is common, and discipline in the home often shows itself as an inconsistent mixture of permissiveness and harshness. Rejection by one or other parent is extremely common. There seems to be a failure of identification of the son with the father in the process of growing-up.

In Britain extreme degrees of poverty and social disorganization are rare, so that the picture of the ghetto-dwelling delinquent youngster, drawn from American studies, has little relevance here. On the other hand two important factors do stand out: these are the clear relevance of age and sex. Boys are in general more delinquent than girls, and the young are more delinquent than the old.

If the official crime statistics are anything to go by, it could well be argued that delinquent behaviour is self-limiting since the number of offences falls off with age. The economic background to crime in this country probably relates to periods of financial hardship rather than to conditions of permanent poverty. For example, someone would be more likely to commit a crime when unemployed than when in work. A further point which has emerged from a large number of studies undertaken both in the United Kingdom and in America is that the delinquent youngster is likely to come from a large family. Belonging to a large family can often mean that a youngster will drift into delinquent acts through lack of adequate supervision. Even if the father is earning a reasonably good wage, supporting a large family is bound to strain his financial resources. The control and training of many children is also harder for the mother, particularly if she is in poor health. The lack of general supervision in large families can be reflected by such indications as the rates of truancy.

It is, of course, important to realize that there is apparently no single cause for criminal behaviour. A large number of studies have been devoted to the social backgrounds, personal characteristics, psychological attributes and so on of young people involved in criminal acts, and certain general observations have emerged. However, it must be conceded that, with the exception of the age and sex factors mentioned earlier, no single factor can be cited to predict criminal behaviour. As West (1967) has commented "although no single type of hardship has a monopoly in relation to delinquency, it could be that delinquents experience an accumulation of adverse pressures which build up to the point where restraints are overcome and crimes occur." It is this sort of balanced statement that is badly needed when considering the juvenile offender.

Given then that young males are more likely to be involved in general delinquent acts than girls, it is hardly surprising that they predominate in the population of drug-users. In England when one looks at the overall rates for delinquency it is clear that in terms of absolute numbers drug offences constitute a very small proportion, albeit an expanding proportion. As already mentioned, a wide range of antisocial behaviour, including sexual assault and attempted murder, has been attributed to people acting under the influence of drugs. It is necessary to return constantly to the myth of the "dope fiend." This is a myth that has been reinforced and popularized by fiction but has little substance in reality. A good example is found in the report of the Indian Hemp Drugs Commission, 1893, which examined a large number of witnesses concerning the physical, moral, and mental effects of taking hashish. In their general conclusions the Commission reported that although many witnesses claimed to have seen violent crimes committed under the influence of hashish, when questioned none of them was able to remember precise details. It is just this sort of anecdote, passed from one person to another, which has credited drugs with the ability to produce violent behaviour in people. Clearly a person who has aggressive tendencies is more likely to behave in an aggressive fashion when under the influence of certain substances – especially of alcohol. There is a very high correlation between alcohol and crimes involving violence, just as there is a very high correlation between alcohol and road-traffic deaths. People intoxicated by alcohol suffer impaired judgement, lowered self-control, and if they are basically prickly and irritable, it is hardly surprising that they may erupt into violent behaviour. In the case of drugs such as opiates the reverse effect is the rule. Opiates in general dull people's behaviour and decrease violent tendencies, sexual propensities, appetite, and thirst. In fact, as long ago as 1925, Lawrence Kolb in America made the point that many aggressive psychopathic individuals would probably improve in temperament under the influence of an opiate-like drug. In parenthesis it should be noted that for at least two hundred years opium was used by medical men as a tranquillizer until its potential dangers were fully appreciated. Even in the case of mind-altering drugs such as lysergic acid there is little solid evidence to support the notion that they induce people to behave in a violent way. Most of the cases studied to date suggest that they have merely intensified pre-existing aggressive tendencies.

The country with the largest problem of delinquency linked with drug use is the United States – possibly a consequence of repressive legislation rather then of drug-use. The introduction of the Harrison Act of 1914 had the indirect effect of placing all drug-users automatically outside the law, and it intensified the reluctance of doctors and social agencies to treat them. The only way in which a drug-user could obtain a drug such as heroin was by illicit means, and in consequence a very intricate system of marketing drugs illicitly has developed, with all the ramifications and complex structure of a large industrial organization. Drugs can be obtained, but at a price. A person whose drug habit costs him 40 dollars a day will need 40 dollars, and the simplest way to acquire 40 dollars if he is out of a job is by theft. Thus theft by drug-users is said to account for something like 70 per cent of the larcenies committed in New York City, and it is estimated that every day approximately a million dollars' worth of property is stolen to provide money to buy drugs. Acts of violence do occur as well – not under the influence of the drug but rather under the indirect influence of the need to procure it; for when the established addict is deprived of the substance he is prepared to go to great lengths to obtain it, particularly if he happens to have an antisocial personality disorder. It would be no understatement to say that repressive anti-drug legislation in the United States has contributed to one of the major social disasters of that country's development. It has intensified the problems of criminality associated with drug-use to a considerable degree – so much so that the trend is unlikely to be reversed merely by making heroin available to all addicts; the problem in the United States is far too large and intricate to be solved by such simple means. Such a situation as has developed in the States should be avoided in other countries at all costs.

The notion that a disturbing and anxiety-provoking problem

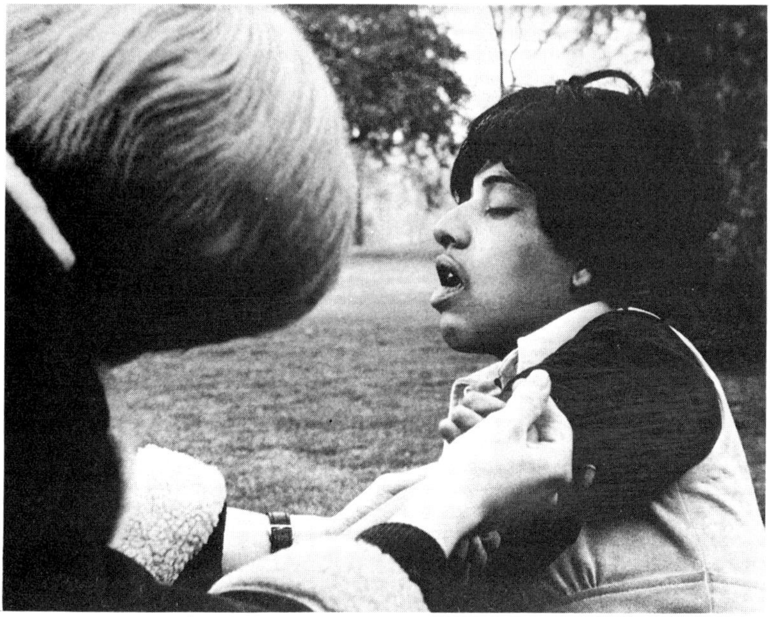

A coloured girl being helped to inject herself with heroin

like drug-use can be dispelled by harsh laws may often seem attractive. Strict legal control suggests that potential drug-users will be deterred and the problem will diminish. However, legislation in the field of drug-use will have the greatest effect if the laws exert some degree of control over the production and distribution of dependency-producing drugs. Such legislation will achieve a certain rational balance between absolute permissiveness and a degree of legal repression. Too much legal repression causes the law to be disregarded and brought into ridicule.

A recent example of over-severe repression was quoted by a judge, William Little of the Ontario Family Court (1969), in a Toronto newspaper which described the case of two people who each received a fourteen-year sentence for importing 150 pounds of marijuana. The columnist had remarked: "It will make no difference. The marijuana habit, which tens of thousands of Canadians find less physically harmful than cigarette-smoking and less socially harmful than drunkenness, will continue without pause and will continue to find more adherents." Yet as the columnist pointed out, in the very same court in that year a man charged with the manslaughter of a welfare-worker was sentenced to two years for assault with the comment from the judge that "everybody is worried about you, son." William Little commented: "On the one hand a dead woman and a two-year sentence; on the other 150 pounds of confiscated marijuana and a fourteen-year sentence. Is this reasonable?"

Since drug-use amongst the young is a relatively new area of concern in Britain the relationship between drug-usage and delinquent behaviour is a field of research for which data is still being collected. In reviewing the cases of heroin-addicts seen in London prisons during 1967, James (1969) reported that three-quarters of these drug-users had a history of court convictions prior to their drug-usage. A common finding was that the addicts had experienced personal and social difficulties since adolescence: they tended to have been youngsters who had dropped out of educational programmes and had had a poor work record. Bewley and Ben-Arie (1968) found that 82 per cent of male heroin-addicts admitted to Tooting Bec Hospital had a previous history of police convictions. In a comparative study, involving subjects from the United Kingdom and the United States and described by Willis (1969), it was found that of forty-two male hospitalized heroin addicts with an average age of 20·4 years, 79 per cent had a previous history of arrest or conviction and 38 per cent had been in prison. In a more recent study by Willis (1970) involving a group of seventy-seven heroin-addicts attending a London treatment centre it was found that while 23·4 per cent had had no arrests or convictions, 47·6 per cent had had between one and four convictions, 24 per cent had had between five and nine, and 23·4 per cent had had over ten. Also 54·5 per cent had been convicted before taking up drugs. The offences involved in these two studies reported by Willis were, in the main, relatively trivial ones involving larceny, absconding, and taking and driving away.

Since society defines drug-use as illicit it is hardly surprising that the more it emerges as a problem in Britain the more it tends to have an appeal for someone with an existing background of delinquency.

Drug-usage and delinquency are both areas which give rise to confusion, but unhappily they are areas where assertions tend to be made without any supporting evidence. It is hardly surprising that when the two become merged, the assertions become wilder and the facts less easy to ascertain.

Unfortunately, most of our information to date is concerned with the drug-using habits of people already identified as delinquent. In the future there is a need for much more information about drug-usage among non-delinquent people. However, it would be a pity if this sort of study were restricted to questionnaires handed out to students at universities, asking them about the nature and frequency of their drug experience. This sort of inquiry, while providing some information about a particular section of the population, is too limited. Inquiries need to be carried out on a much broader scale. The difficulties in undertaking them in this highly sensitive area are, of course, enormous. Nevertheless, the information is badly needed.

Chapter 9

The treatment of alcoholism and drug-dependence

In this chapter it is intended to describe the basic principles of treatment for alcoholism and drug-dependence. A more detailed examination of methods of treatment would be inappropriate in a work whose purpose is to present only a general overall view.

First of all it is necessary to state the basic philosophy of treatment. Treatment of any disorder is aimed at reversing or halting a basic disease process and any complications that may be involved. In some instances this may be relatively simple, as with healing a fractured bone, removing a diseased appendix, or curing pneumonia with antibiotics. But with less tangible disorders, which involve changes in feeling and conduct, we find that notion of "treatment" becomes less clear. In the whole area of psychiatric treatment we find that "cure" is not easy and that prognosis may be imprecise.

The goals and results of psychiatric treatment are not easily defined, because knowledge is generally insufficient and too often overshadowed by the biases and prejudices of professionals who really ought to know better. In the treatment of alcoholism and drug-dependence we find the same confusion, the same lack of clarity, and the same tendency to replace solid facts by opinion and untested hypotheses. Further difficulties arise because treatment of alcoholism and drug-dependence tends to get involved with matters of public policy. One might define policy as the sane conducting of public affairs, and of course there *are* large areas relating to health and disease prevention where policy lines can properly be laid down. Examples are the notification of infectious diseases, treatment of tuberculosis, vaccination, immunization – a host of aspects of public health that are vital to the welfare of the nation. On the whole, health problems for which a line of policy may be dictated tend to be covered by a satisfactory background of knowledge. In the case of alcoholism, policy lines at the moment just about merit consideration as coherent expressions of informed opinion. But in the case of drug-dependence and drug-abuse, factual knowledge of causation, even of the very nature of dependence, is so unclear and contentious that it is really not possible to make any clear policy statements except those relating to the manufacture and control of drugs or those likely to prevent illicit traffic and sale. Even here there is disagreement over substances such as cannabis. So the public is not to blame if, unaware of the real lack of expert knowledge, it supports legislation based on faulty information given by self-appointed experts. Nor for that matter are legislators to be blamed if they construct laws based on faulty information. Senior administrators and civil servants can only act on the information which is made available to them.

On a more personal level we find important difficulties regarding treatment of the alcohol- or drug-abuser. Frequently people, professionals included, seem unaware that these disorders so far show both a high relapse-rate and a tendency to become chronic conditions. Besides, they are disorders which carry a stigma which, no doubt, is related to their social effects. This can lead medical men to eschew proper investigation and treatment of such patients, encouraged by a vague notion that the alcoholic or the drug-user is blameworthy, that his problems arise from a "weak character" which renders him morally and socially inferior to his fellows and therefore less in need or deserving of treatment. Of course it must be remarked that in treating such patients one should steer a clear course between the extremes of paternalistic authoritarianism and woolly-minded permissiveness. A good starting point for treatment is to recognize that these disorders are likely to be long-term.

The treatment of chronic disorders forms a large area of medical practice. There are few chronic illnesses that cannot at least be palliated and the sufferer and family encouraged – a fact which often tends to be overlooked. In any out-patient clinic at a general hospital we can find physicians and surgeons providing long-term care for people with chronic disorders for which there may be no dramatic relief (despite the truly remarkable advances made in treatment during the twentieth century). Medical and nursing professionals manage to cope very well with

A drug-addict talking matters over with a specialist in his home environment

chronic illness, without too much misgiving. So the negative reactions evoked by alcoholics and drug-users may seem incongruous until we recall how easily these disorders are blamed on weakness or vicious self-indulgence. At the same time it is wrong to be too lofty about this: the behaviour of alcoholics and drug-users *does* have personal and social consequences. The drug-user may all too often be importunate and demanding, and it would take a person of saintly altruism or near psychotic insensitivity to be either unaware of or unaffected by this. But this should not deter society from rational attempts at investigation and treatment.

On a deeper personal level we should recognize that alcohol- and drug-use in patients may even provoke the doctor's own anxieties about these substances. Alcohol is in common use, and there can be few reasonably intelligent people who are regular social drinkers who have never had misgivings about their own ability to cope with alcohol. Thus doctors and nurses might feel genuinely threatened by inklings of themselves that they may see in patients who abuse alcohol or drugs. The seemingly intractable nature of the complaint may make doctors and nurses wary of a disorder which interweaves so closely with the "normal." Perhaps then it is not so surprising that drink and drugs generate heat and emotion. Medical people have access to drugs in their work – it is no coincidence that doctors and nurses form a hard core of any drug-dependent population. For example, sleep disturbance due to night work is a common starting-point for nurses to misuse such drugs as barbiturates.

The unwillingness of many alcohol- or drug-users to accept treatment also causes difficulties, especially since in other types of disorder the patient is only too keen to have treatment and to co-operate fully (to much greater degree than is perhaps generally recognized).

GENERAL TREATMENT

Whether the patient is dependent on drugs or alcohol, certain basic principles of treatment are valid. The most important of these arise from the reasonable assumption that the addict or alcoholic often arrives at a stage in the natural history of his disorder where he is suffering actual damage as a result of his use. This may seem a naïve statement but it needs setting down in black and white. We distinguish between normal and abnormal drinking. The normal drinker we would regard as someone with control over his alcohol intake: neither his physique nor personal and social life are in any way endangered by his use of alcohol. Now here there is a very real difference between alcoholics and drug-addicts. Social drinking is widespread, but we cannot really accept that there is such a thing as normal and casual drug-use. This may be a contentious point but perhaps it should be aired a little. The drugs on which people become dependent tend to be powerful and dangerous ones whose subjective effects are striking. Further, the rate of becoming dependent on them is likely to be rapid. Though some people may develop states of drug-dependence quite slowly, generally the process is fairly quick. Alcohol-dependence, however, is likely to take a period of years to develop, though recent experiments show that, providing they take enough, people can become quite severely physically dependent on alcohol in a short period of time.

Any study of the treatment of drug-dependence is a constant reiteration of catalogues of pure misery and wretchedness, and not necessarily in dramatic or colourful terms either. Inevitably the testimony of drug-users suggests that the immediate, short-term benefits and pleasures received from drugs are fairly soon replaced by long intervals of personal and social disability. It is unfortunate that the use of drugs has acquired a meretricious and glamorous mystique which is at variance with the real facts.

Thus the assumption that alcohol and drugs are eventually damaging to people is reasonable, and so the basic object of treatment is to help the alcohol- or drug-user to live in the world as it is without the need for alcohol or drugs. This certainly remains a constant goal in treatment, particularly in the case of the drug-user, but it must be acknowledged that total abstention for every patient is often unrealistic as a primary goal of treatment. Nevertheless the good sense in working towards eventual total abstention remains unchallenged.

WITHDRAWAL FROM ALCOHOL AND DRUGS

Alcohol

Withdrawal from alcohol is usually arranged in a hospital. The reasons for this are simple: in hospital it is easier to supervise withdrawal and guard against its risks. An important hazard with alcohol-withdrawal is the development of states of restlessness and tremulous excitement known as delirium tremens (the DTs). At one time this condition entailed a high mortality-rate but this was probably mainly due to the states of physical self-neglect of the patient and to the fact that in those days general standards of medical care were poor. Nowadays the alcoholic, no matter how much he drinks, can be detoxified from alcohol relatively easily, and states of delirium can be calmed. Undernourishment and neglect are treated with feeding and sensible medical care and a generous intake of fluids. Severe cases of alcoholism often show signs of vitamin shortage and so nowadays large doses of vitamins are given during alcohol withdrawal, particularly vitamins of the B group. This can counteract the development of states of excitement and prevent damage to the nervous system. At the same time the patient's general physical state is evaluated and any complications are diagnosed and treated.

Drugs

Many suppose that withdrawal from drugs is always a dramatic and terrifying experience. In fact, though the symptoms may be severe, withdrawal is easily supervised: good medical and nursing care makes it easy. The drug-user often shows signs of severe self-neglect, so his admission to hospital is used as an opportunity to evaluate this during the withdrawal period. The withdrawal procedure is carried out by gradually reducing doses of the drug over a period of days or weeks. Nowadays withdrawal from opiate-like drugs is made easier by the use of methadone (physeptone), a slowly-absorbed drug with prolonged action. Some distress is inevitable but it should be remembered that drug users may overstate their symptoms. Good medical and nursing care backed up by the use of methadone can make opiate-withdrawal comparatively easy.

Real dangers occur in cases of withdrawal from barbiturates, since heavy users of barbiturates often develop withdrawal fits. They are withdrawn by reducing doses throughout a period of days. Stimulant drugs such as the amphetamines need no replacement and are stopped straightaway. Psychological distress may be a source of great complaint in amphetamine-users but on the whole they tend to become very drowsy when the drugs are stopped and they recover spontaneously.

AFTER WITHDRAWAL

The real problems begin after withdrawal. Relapse rates are high, so people tend to look for magical treatment methods which will somehow sweep away the errors and disappointments of past cures. But it is possible to adopt a rational attitude to treatment without being overwhelmed by it all. Where alcohol or drugs are concerned the general principle is to try to educate the patient to become aware of the full implications of his disability, and to look for ways of encouraging abstention. At this point there is a difference between what can be done for the alcoholic and what can be done for the drug-user. This difference is related less to the pharmacological action of the substances involved and more to the attitudes of society towards drugs and alcohol, for a relapsed drinker faces very different reactions than does a relapsed drug-user.

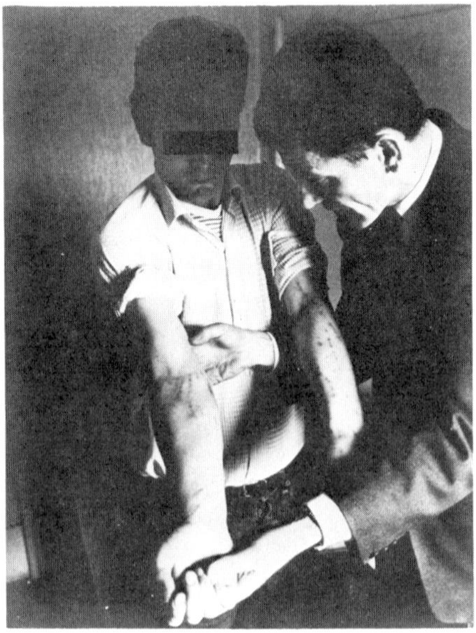

Inspecting the "tracks"

REHABILITATION OF THE ALCOHOLIC PATIENT

Many alcoholics tell a clear story of attempts at abstention: some are successful for weeks or months, many are unsuccessful. The latter may be discouraged by their failure and feel guilty and ashamed. Many alcoholics are likely to become severely depressed. Here the task of the doctor is to treat the depression, but nevertheless there remains the basic problem of the person's difficulty in handling alcohol. Events of crucial importance psychologically, such as a religious conversion or getting married, may exert a great stabilizing influence. I am not prescribing marriage or religion as a cure for alcoholism, but people can undergo profound psychological change independent of "treatment." Some alcoholics just stop drinking once they realize the real extent of their problem. An example of this was of a fifty-two-year-old man who was referred to an out-patient clinic for the investigation of alcoholism. He had been drinking heavily for ten years, with a history of uncontrolled drinking for the past five years. In that time his health deteriorated and he became physically dependent on alcohol. It was thought that little could be done without admission to hospital and out-patient follow-up. He refused to go into hospital, saying that he had a lifelong fear of such places. This was thought to be a defence against treatment on his part, so the patient's family doctor and the hospital doctor were insistent that he should follow their advice. He said "I am able to do this on my own and I will." In fact, he did. He was reluctant to come to the out-patient clinic again and wrote letters from time to time, and eventually turned up a year later completely transformed, totally abstinent from alcohol, and able to cope with his life in a far more sensible and reasonable way.

TREATMENT OF THE ALCOHOLIC PATIENT

Psychological Methods

Group treatment seems to be of help to the alcoholic patient: he is confronted with the realities of his situation in the company of other alcoholics. The use of treatment in groups derives not so much from a lack of success in individual treatment as from the discovery that alcoholics can learn from the experience of others who have been through similar situations. They can talk about their problems and realize that they are not unique, and that their attempts at self-deception, the stratagems they employ to conceal alcohol dependence from themselves, are tricks which have been used by thousands before them. In the group, abrasive criticism and a high emotional climate are commonplace, and these produce displays of feeling that lead to greater self-awareness. The group can give support and encouragement and teach the alcoholic the real meaning of alcohol.

Nowadays, hospital alcoholic units tend to work in co-operation with the organization called Alcoholics Anonymous. Alcoholics Anonymous is widely known: it was founded before the Second World War by two American professional men who were themselves both alcoholics. The basic philosophy of Alcoholics Anonymous is full of good sense. It asks of the alcoholic a sense of commitment and involvement in an ongoing process of self-realization, plus the crucial recognition that for the alcoholic alcohol is always potentially dangerous. With this comes a realization that he is not alone and can expect the support of fellow-members of Alcoholics Anonymous at any time. These guiding principles have brought enormous help and comfort to numerous alcoholics and their families.

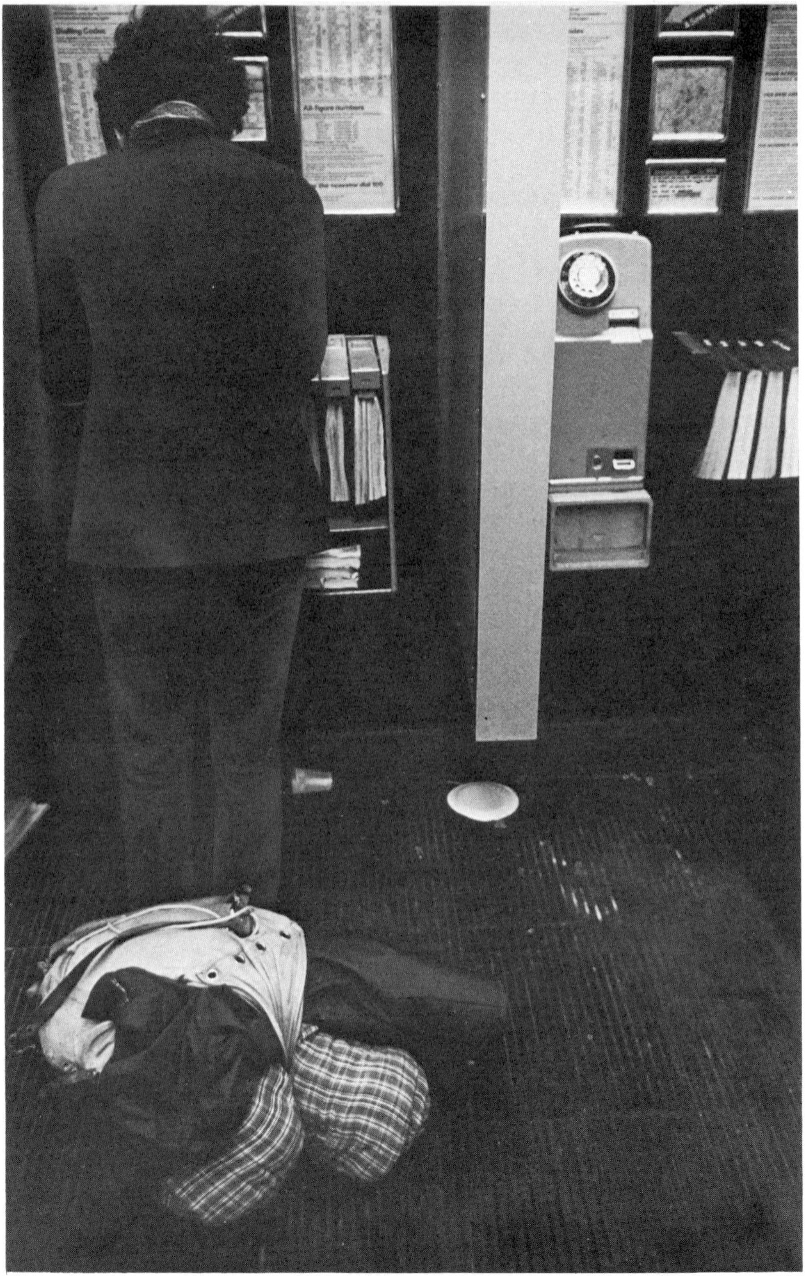

Alcoholics Anonymous may be contacted at any time by someone in need

Medication and the Treatment of Alcoholism

Medication and treatment are difficult since many fear the risks of giving drugs to the alcoholic. In general the use of sedatives is discouraged. On the other hand the use of tranquillizing drugs does have some value for a tense or anxious alcoholic though many feel this treatment should not be continued for too long. The most widely-known drug that has been used in the treatment of alcoholism is disulfiram (Antabuse). This drug causes profound and frightening side-effects for the alcoholic if he drinks alcohol whilst taking it. Many regard it as just an easy way out. This scorn is understandable, but in fact disulfiram has proved itself very useful in the treatment of alcoholism. No one suggests it should be the treatment chosen for all, but rather that it may be used for many. A careful consideration of possible treatments always looks at the full range of methods available rather than tries to impose the same plan of treatment on everyone.

THE RECIDIVIST DRINKER

Whatever else may be said about the treatment of alcoholism it is true that recidivist drinkers create many problems. These are people who just go on drinking despite attempts at treatment and after periods of apparent co-operativeness. They are often in and out of prison for drunkenness. They represent a great burden on the public health, both in the United Kingdom and in the United States, and by sheer numbers they present more of a public-health problem than do drug-users. Repeated imprisonment is not much use in dealing with them, nor is repeated hospitalization except for periods of "drying out." Such people may slide down the social scale and gradually take to cheaper but stronger forms of alcohol such as rough cider and surgical spirits. They remain in a state of chronic intoxication and suffer from malnutrition, physical illnesses and general neglect. Their appearance is often unattractive and unkempt, and when drunk they may be rowdy, noisy and aggressive. Nowadays some people think such recidivists might be helped by community-based hostels but, as the experts point out, it is no use opening up a hostel, filling it with recidivist drinkers and hoping for the best.

Hostels need to be carefully run by wardens of sufficient flexibility and patience to tolerate the difficulty of looking after their charges. Many of these men have not worked regularly for years, except for spells of casual work, and so social rehabilitation is often a lengthy process, sometimes ineffectual, and mostly full of disappointments. In hostels it would be possible to support these patients for longer terms in a more organized state than if they were sleeping rough and wandering about the streets. Like so many chronic disorders, recidivist alcoholism is one where the results of any treatment are better than complete neglect. Community-based hostels for the alcoholic can slow down the downward trend and halt a dreary cycle which may involve return to prison. If they can do this they have achieved a worthwhile, though no doubt unspectacular, degree of success.

PROPHYLAXIS AND EDUCATION

Government prohibition of alcohol has achieved no success. Somehow we will have to compromise with the problem of alcohol, but hopefully we could avoid some of the pitfalls by relatively simple measures. Excessive advertising of alcohol in glamorous and seductive terms is something that really should be stopped. At the same time people should be warned about the dangers of alcohol. This is more likely to be achieved by practical rather than histrionic means. No doubt we need to teach youngsters at an early age the very real dangers they may run into with drinking, and whilst making them aware of alcohol educate them in its sensible use.

THE TREATMENT OF DRUG-DEPENDENCE

After withdrawal from drugs the patient usually feels better and has increased confidence in his ability to stay away from them, even though he may have suffered speedy relapses after previous withdrawal sessions. If treatment is to mean anything at all and relapse is to be avoided, it should be possible to offer some help to the patient in the period after withdrawal. If he is then left on his own to go out into the community unaided, and so relapses quickly, it could be thought almost cruel to have offered him withdrawal in the first place with nothing to back it up.

The bulk of experience in long-term treatment of drug-dependence has been acquired in America through treatment of heroin-users. It is not possible to apply a set of findings from one country to another but a great deal of practical good sense can be learnt from American experience. Perhaps the first point to be emphasized is the enormous problem presented by the very real change in social outlook and behaviour that the drug-user is likely to have undergone – particularly if over the years he has moved completely into the society of drug-users and assimilated their attitudes, values and life-style. When he leaves hospital he is likely to experience a strong inclination to return to drugs, whereas in the absence of drugs the users' outlook on life will have to change, since his previous life-style was drug-oriented. Thus some other constructive life-style needs to be adopted. Certainly, long-term incarceration in institutions such as prisons and hospitals achieves little on its own.

In recent years it has been realized that many drug-users can be helped by therapy which involves former drug-users. The first example of this was Synanon, an organization started in America. It was founded by a former alcoholic who became aware of the difficulties facing drug-users. The object of the Synanon method is to put the user in a position where he has to look at himself and his previous way of life in an intensive and stark fashion. Someone entering a Synanon house commits himself to the rules and obligations of that society and is expected to learn to behave as a responsible person, on the assumption (usually correct) that heretofore he has been behaving irresponsibly. He must learn that his drug-use is unacceptable, and he is given the opportunity of learning to live a drug-free life, with help from the Synanon community: he must be able to accept not only its support but also its censure and hostility where needed. He starts off at the lowest rung of the ladder and by co-operating he must prove that he can behave properly and achieve some rise in his status within the Synanon house.

This approach to rehabilitation of drug-use has been developed elsewhere, notably in New York in such places as Day Top Lodge and the Phoenix Houses. Here the emphasis is constantly on vigorous group interaction and the use of techniques such as encounter groups, where patients are encouraged to display their pent-up feelings, but only at prescribed times. The rest of the time they must live in co-operation within the society under the influence and guidance of counsellors who were themselves formerly drug-users.

The general approach of these groups is to demand of the addict a strong commitment to the idea of living in a world without drugs, and to make him realize that he must transform himself from the passive role of being cushioned against life by drug-use, into a more active and positive role where he must bear responsibility for his actions and be aware how they affect others. It is hoped that he will thereby achieve mature insight into the significance of his personal relationships. He must learn to stop manipulating people for his own gratification, and above all he must learn very clearly just what damage he has been doing to himself through his former behaviour.

The philosophy of this type of rehabilitation programme is basically one of informed and sophisticated self-help, wherein drug-use is recognized as an infantile way of coming to terms with the world. The patient's stay in such communities is usually lengthy, if anything is to be achieved, and for this reason not every drug-user will find them acceptable. No one would suggest that he should, though group therapy seems a vigorous and positive way of helping people. Experience of its use in this country is as yet limited, but it seems that encouraging beginnings are being made.

PHARMACOLOGICAL METHODS IN THE TREATMENT OF DRUG-DEPENDENCE

The main use of tranquillizers and sedatives for drug-users has really only the short-term aim of alleviating periods of distress. Regular medication is hazardous, whether it be with anti-depressants or tranquillizers. In recent years there has been great interest in the use of methadone as a "blockade" drug for the heroin-user. The addict using methadone is often seen as someone with a severe physical dependence on heroin, or too frequently as someone for whom all varieties of treatment, psychological and otherwise, have failed, and someone suffering less from a psychological disorder than from a state of prolonged biochemical dependence on heroin.

The originators of methadone maintenance treatment (Dole,

1965) view it as a way of "blocking" the craving for drugs and preventing the patient from becoming euphoric if he should take them. Methadone is given in high doses orally once a day under supervision and patients are carefully followed up with regular urine-screening. No one is suggesting that this is the answer to every such case, but with some patients – possibly a high percentage – it may prove a very important beginning. For it gives the opportunity of rehabilitation and re-entry into society, while protecting the patient from a desire to find drugs.

Sadly one senses an atmosphere of almost professional rivalry between advocates of one form or another of the long-term treatment for drug-users. No one has the corner on expertise in the treatment of these patients: present knowledge suggests that rational empiricism is what is most needed.

THE MAINTENANCE TREATMENT OF DRUG-USERS – "THE BRITISH SYSTEM"

For many years it was supposed that our special system, "The British System," of legally prescribing drugs for people dependent on them, had in some way prevented the spread of drug-dependence in this country. However, on examination it was realized that this was not exactly the case. What was apparent was that over the years the problem of drug-dependence had never been very great, and, this being the case, it had been regarded as humane and acceptable to prescribe narcotic drugs for users where it was felt that their history was one of repeated treatment failure. In a sense this system probably worked relatively well for such a small number of patients whose drug problem was very much their own and presented few social problems to others. However, with the upsurge in heroin-dependence it became clear that the system of prescribing heroin for the user now needed revaluation. This position has been clearly reviewed by Connell (1967, 1970) who has shown that uncontrolled prescribing of narcotic drugs on a "maintenance" basis is unworkable. Any attempt to prescribe narcotics on such a basis needs to be carefully controlled and supervised: in this way it is hoped to avoid creating new addicts, and also the possibility of the user passing on any of his prescribed dose to others.

The legal prescribing of heroin for the drug-user is perhaps

Registered addicts can usually obtain their drugs from retail pharmacists such as this one at Piccadilly Circus

best regarded as a social measure since its object is to avoid the establishment of an illicit market. But it should be realized that there is a very real difference between prescribing heroin for, say, a middle-aged person who has been taking it for years, and prescribing it on a maintenance basis for a youngster of seventeen who comes to a clinic after using the drug for only a few months.

There is no doubt, too, that the prescribing of drugs for drug-users presents real moral problems for the doctors involved. They may feel they are colluding in a self-destructive process. At present the whole procedure of prescribing narcotic drugs to addicts in this country is being carefully evaluated, but it is too early to offer any useful comments about the likely outcome. At the moment the prescription system appears a basically humane practice, but one needing careful appraisal and honest examination of the results with the passage of time.

Chapter 10

The law in relation to drugs and alcohol

Legal proceedings concerning drugs and alcohol are extensive, complicated, and sometimes baffling. Perhaps this is not surprising. Society makes its laws with an eye to the general welfare, to protect the rights of the individual, and deter the would-be offender, and these aims may sometimes conflict. It would be naïve to expect perfection from the law any more than from any other human endeavour. It may be more appropriate to regard laws as pragmatic expressions of society's needs and expectations, which are usually formulated through a democratic process of deliberation and debate. The countries with the most humane and workable legal systems are those where legal constraints are decided by common sense and discussion rather than rigid decrees.

In fact one great strength of the legal system in Britain is that the laws can be modified by practice and experience. But laws concerning drugs and alcohol present certain difficulties since modifications to them tend to be made only after the social problems caused by drugs and alcohol have already become apparent, and when it is too late to prevent them. Nevertheless there is a degree of good sense in many of these legal measures.

Let us first examine the laws relating to drunkenness. The legal associations of "inebriety," from the Latin *in* (intensive) and *ebrietas* (drunkenness) are partly civil and partly criminal. As regards civil responsibilities, it is perfectly possible when drunk to make a valid will, or to enter into a valid marriage, to bind oneself by contract, providing one retains enough sobriety to recognize the implications, and providing also that no one takes advantage of one's condition. The position is not quite so clear as regards criminal responsibility. In Britain the basic assumption of the law is that a man is always responsible for his actions and should therefore be liable for their consequences. This means that arguments about responsibility are concerned with the degree of intent: in other words whether it can be established beyond all reasonable doubt that the person *intended* the result of his actions and should therefore be held responsible for them. The topic of criminal responsibility is notoriously contentious and is really beyond the scope of this book, but without some reference to it no discussion of the criminal aspects of drugs and alcohol is complete.

Four principles need to be considered here. Firstly, the law assumes a man is responsible for his actions and intends their consequences. Secondly, it is presumed that a man is sane, so that the presence of insanity must be proved before it can be accepted in mitigation. Thirdly, it is held that criminal responsibility is founded on intention as well as action; this is expressed in the legal maxim *actus non facit reum nisi mens sit rea* ("There cannot be a guilty act unless there is a guilty mind"). Lastly there is the important principle that no one can be deprived of his liberty or suffer any interference with his right to manage his own affairs on purely medical or psychiatric grounds. This is an important safeguard for the individual. Where such steps to interfere are taken at the instigation of doctors they must always be backed up by an appointed representative acting for the individual, whether this be a relative or a social-worker duly recognized by law.

It is usually in cases of violent, inexplicable crime such as murder that a person's responsibility is questioned, and this was very much the case when murder was still a capital offence.

In the last century many judges recognized that there must sometimes be doubt about true responsibility for acts of murder, but no formal legal decision was made until 1834 with the case of Daniel McNaghten, who killed the Prime Minister's secretary. He was later acquitted on the grounds of insanity; after the trial fifteen English judges were asked to answer five questions set for them by the House of Lords in the belief that their response would clarify the true definition of criminal responsibility. In time the embodiment of the answers to four of these five questions came to be known as the McNaghten rules. These rules can be interpreted as follows: a defence of insanity was possible if it could be proved "that at the time of committing the act the accused was labouring under such a defect of reason from disease of mind as not to know the nature and quality of the act he was doing; or if he knew what he was doing, that he did not know that it was wrong." Initially, no doubt, the McNaghten rules seemed to clarify the position, but in practice they were difficult to apply and aroused legal and medical discontent. For it was recognized that people could develop severe illnesses which might prompt them to act occasionally in an uncharacteristic manner, and yet in the eyes of the law they could be held responsible for such acts. With the passage of time the concept of diminished responsibility was accepted; in this country it found expression in the Homicide Act of 1957, which recognized it as a mitigating factor able to reduce a charge of capital murder to one of culpable homicide.

The relevance of all this to alcohol and drugs lies in the fact that people's behaviour can change quite drastically under the influence of either of these substances. Thus if the person was intoxicated when charged with a criminal offence it may be thought he was less than responsible for his actions. In the case of alcohol there is a dilemma. On the one hand drunkenness is not regarded as an excuse for criminal behaviour, but on the other hand if someone is drunk while committing an offence it is held that drunkenness can diminish his capacity to form intent. Also juries may take drunkenness into account in considering whether an act was premeditated, or whether someone acted in self-defence or under provocation. Perhaps the situation may be summed up by saying that in the eyes of the law the effect of drugs or alcohol may, to some degree, alter the person's responsibility but does not entirely eliminate it.

So much for the individual. Now for the ways in which society uses its laws to control the use of alcohol and drugs.

ALCOHOL

In general the law makes a distinction between private and public drunkenness. Private drunkenness is not an offence but public drunkenness may be. Somebody found drunk in public may be charged with committing a breach of the peace, insulting behaviour, assault, or for causing a variety of disturbances. For many years it was often difficult to prove in practice whether

Customs officials in London discover £500,000 worth of cannabis concealed under the floor-boards of a Swedish lorry (The illegal smuggling operation had originated in Kabul, Afghanistan)

somebody was so drunk as to be incapable of properly driving a motor vehicle. This question has now been resolved by the legal assumption that a person's competence to drive is impaired by having a blood alcohol level in excess of 80 mg per cent. Although there has been much argument over this question, in fact the bulk of scientific evidence supports measurement of the blood-alcohol level as an effective means of estimating driving capability.

Perhaps the most important aspects of the laws on alcohol concern restrictions on the sale of alcoholic drinks. People may complain about the licensing hours in this country, but it must be clearly recognized that legal control of the sale of alcohol represented a valuable social reform, coming as it did after more than a century of severe alcohol abuse by vast sections of the population. Although there is no doubt that the heavy drinking of the eighteenth and nineteenth centuries was very clearly associated with extreme social deprivation and hopelessness, there is also no doubt that the easy availability of cheap strong spirits was a crucial factor in the spread of alcohol abuse. Though often criticized and no doubt containing anomalies, our licensing laws are still the product of a sensible spirit of social reform.

A canister, believed to contain cannabis, being removed for inspection

DRUGS

As in the case of alcohol, the history of attempts at legal control of drug-use is one of retrospective rather then prospective legislation, since the laws tend to be passed when the dangers of these drugs have already become apparent. Thus the laws do not, in general, attempt to forestall the dangers. We know that there certainly are inconsistencies and anomalies in the laws relating to drugs, but such shortcomings should not blind us to the fact that certain drugs are dangerous, so that society must enforce some regulations to control their manufacture, storage, distribution and usage.

Some people consider that the use of drugs is entirely a matter for the individual and should concern no one else, but this takes too narrow a view of human existence; for there are very few people so socially isolated that their actions do not impinge on the lives of others. After all, no one calls into question the laws governing the sale and storage of highly dangerous poisons such as strychnine and arsenic. Whilst the effects of dependency-producing drugs may not be so dramatic and violent as those of severe poisons, yet most people would agree that these drugs are dangerous and there is good sense in attempting to impose some degree of control over them by means of national and international law.

In the United Kingdom the Dangerous Drugs Act, 1964 and 1965, covers the production, sales, storage, prescription and possession of highly potent and dependency-producing drugs. The range of drugs included in this category is extensive, involving over eighty drugs altogether. They cover the following: medicinal opium; opiates and derivatives such as morphine and diamorphine; synthetic pain-relieving drugs whose action is opiate-like, as pethidine and methadone; cocaine and its derivatives; and any extract or tincture of cannabis. In fact all this legislation will be superseded by the Misuse of Drugs Bill (1971) which categorizes drugs of abuse and alters penalties for infringement of the law as well as empowering the Home Secretary to add new-found drugs of abuse to legal control. The main area of controversy here concerns the inclusion of cannabis in legal control since it is argued that this drug does not produce the physical dependence associated with the other dangerous drugs. On the face of it, it does seem unreasonable for someone taking cannabis to be subject to the same kind of penalty if detected.

The inclusion of cannabis among the dangerous drugs goes back to the 1920s, when the South African government suggested that it should be treated as a dangerous habit-forming drug and brought under international control. This was discussed by the opium advisory committee of the League of Nations which in 1925 asked various governments throughout the world to give information about the production and the use of cannabis. In the League of Nations' opium conference the Egyptian representative set out a memorandum describing the ways in which hashish

Behind the scenes at Interpol: files contain details of thousands of suspects

was prepared and used, and also its possible dangers through acute and chronic intoxication. Apparently the Egyptian delegate made strong requests that cannabis should be put under international control. In the debate that followed other delegates, including those of the United States, China, Great Britain, and France, felt unable to commit their particular country, though in general they sympathized with the concern shown by the Egyptians. Subsequently they reached a unanimous agreement that the whole question should be reviewed and a committee was appointed to look into it. Although it appears that the evidence offered at the time was inconclusive by present-day standards, cannabis was eventually included in the scheme. Of course this was during a period of flux relating to the whole question of establishing international control over known dependency-producing drugs. It is possibly true that cannabis was

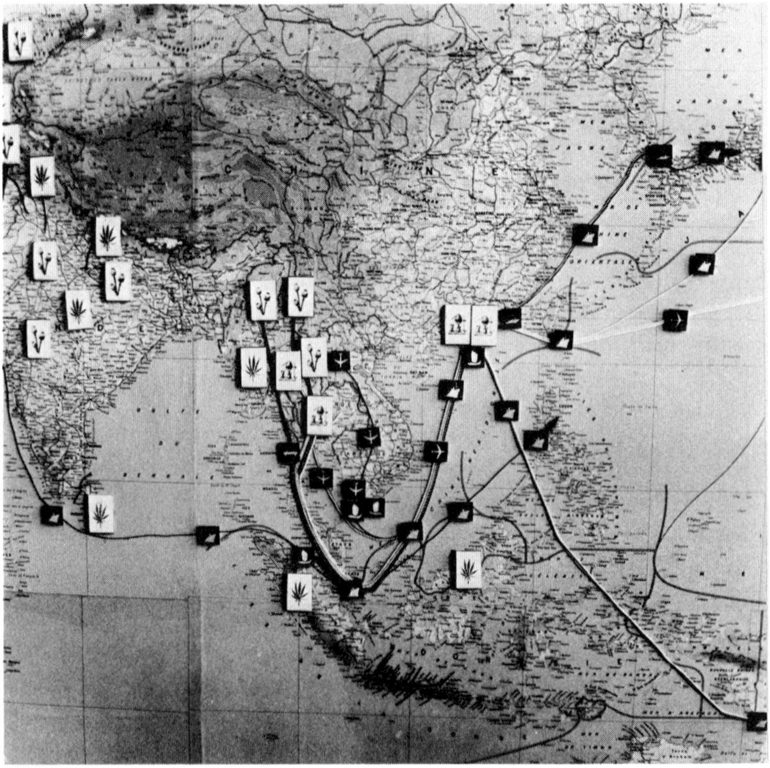

White flags indicate locations where drugs are produced; black flags indicate methods of conveyance

included for reasons considerably more slender than those applying to the opiates.

Perhaps it should be pointed out that the question of exerting international control over narcotic drugs is a comparatively recent one. It arose in 1909 with a conference held in Shanghai where discussions centred round the problem of controlling the use of opium in China. Thereafter, in 1912, the Hague Convention agreed that opium-smoking should be suppressed and that narcotics should only be manufactured for strictly medical uses. By stages in 1920, 1924, and 1925 when the Geneva Convention was signed, the whole problem of international control became more clearly defined.

Proceedings continued over the years until the present time when countries throughout the world co-operate through the United Nations and the World Health Organization in maintaining a mutually agreed system of control over dangerous drugs. In 1961 the United Kingdom was one of the signatories of what is usually called the Single Convention of Narcotic Drugs – a further step in rationalizing the whole procedure. Cannabis is included in the scope of the Single Convention, but at the present time pressure is mounting to have it removed from the list of drugs covered. While it is true that cannabis does not have such dangerous dependency-producing characteristics as the other drugs listed, there is no doubt that the experience of hashish-producing countries has not been a happy one, and that a good deal of social disability and distress has been caused by its chronic use. Perhaps it should be emphasized that the removal of cannabis from the list of "dangerous" drugs does not mean that this will "legalize pot." Legalization is an entirely different matter which will now be examined.

SHOULD CANNABIS BE LEGALIZED?

In the Western world, particularly in America and the United Kingdom, cannabis seems to invite extreme expressions of opinion. On one side there are those who regard cannabis as an inherently seductive and evil substance, and at the other extreme are those who regard it as an entirely harmless intoxicant that should be freely available to all. But this latter opinion takes too simple a view. Taken in low concentrations cannabis is a mild intoxicant whose effect is initially similar to that of alcohol. But in higher concentrations it becomes a stimulating substance capable of evoking psychotic reactions. Although its long-term effects are ever the subject of discussion and speculation, there is at least a widespread consensus of opinion crediting cannabis with the ability to produce chronic conditions wherein the user becomes inert and socially non-productive, so that he neglects himself and his family and deteriorates physically. This may not be due to the direct intoxication produced by the drug but rather to its long-term capacity to deprive the user of energy and drive, resulting in social and physical deterioration.

However, many disagree with this opinion and suggest that these apparent effects are mainly due to the malnutrition and poverty already existing in countries where cannabis-usage is common, as in Egypt and India. This view seems to be largely speculative, and the experience of those who live and work in the countries concerned cannot be dismissed so lightly. At the least, cannabis is a substance which causes occasional states of mild intoxication, sometimes states of severe intoxication, and even, perhaps, states of chronic intoxication.

In spite of this it may be argued that cannabis should not be included in the list of dangerous drugs coming under international control, since it is not a highly dangerous dependency-producing drug. It does not produce any physical dependence, although psychological dependence can occur. Some people have therefore put forward the view that cannabis should be made widely available, since it is not physically addictive. Such a view is surely irrelevant, for cocaine and the amphetamines both produce psychological dependence without physical dependence – yet no one would dispute the very real dangers of these drugs. And for that matter, the majority of chronic alcoholics have no physical dependence either; yet their psychological dependency is such that the whole fabric of their existence is transformed. Hence there is no logical justification for considering that a substance is all right merely because it does not induce physical dependence. Furthermore, although physical dependence on smoking is not very common, psychological dependence is frequently considerable. Yet no one would regard tobacco-smoking as harmless on the grounds that it does not produce any physical dependence.

Another argument sometimes advanced in favour of making cannabis freely available is that there is no evidence of its causing damage to body or brain. Again, this is irrelevant, for any declaration based on negative findings must be suspect. A more important point, however, is that with cannabis, as with other drugs, the long-term effects are often more manifest in their social consequences for the individual as opposed to the mere physical harm they may do to him.

A further argument that is made in favour of the free availability of cannabis is that it has no direct causal link with the individual's moving on to more dangerous drugs, such as heroin. No doubt this is true, but it would be foolish to recommend the use of cannabis to anyone in the confident expectation that this would entail a *lowered* risk of involvement with a stronger drug such as heroin.

A plea for legalizing the use of cannabis, at the "Legalize Pot" rally in Hyde Park, London

Yet another plea for the free use of cannabis is based on the proposition that it causes neither psychotic reactions nor criminal behaviour. Unfortunately our present understanding of the causes of psychosis is so slender that it is hard to countenance any such definite statement. And as to criminal behaviour, the links between cannabis and delinquency are far from clear.

Many people have advanced the theory that cannabis is made attractive by its very illegality, and yet it is less harmful than alcohol. And so, they say, if the law were changed, cannabis would lose an element of its appeal, while the use of it would be less of a problem than the alcohol it would supersede. Therefore, they argue, legalize cannabis and clamp down on alcohol. But active suppression of alcohol has so far been strikingly unsuccessful. In Western society cannabis is a new substance and we have had less than a hundred years' experience of it – a short time in the history of substance abuse. It is oversimple to say that cannabis is less harmful then alcohol. It would be truer to say it is harmful but in different ways.

There is absolutely no evidence at all to suggest that cannabis usage would become less common if it were freely available. Further, one is tempted to ask why countries where its use has long been prevalent have deemed it necessary to legislate against it. As for the argument that cannabis might replace alcohol if it were freely available, again it is difficult to find any justification. Alcoholism is a problem involving very many millions of people in the Western world: it is hard to see how this problem could be eradicated merely by allowing the availability of cannabis. The history of substance-abuse suggests that instead of replacing alcohol we would merely be adding yet another intoxicant to those already available.

Enumeration of the foregoing points is not intended to suggest that the author is either "pro" or "anti" cannabis. Many of the statements made in the past about the supposed ill-effects of cannabis have been just as fallacious as most of the arguments advanced in favour of its free usage. It was a mistake to include cannabis in the category of a dangerous narcotic dependency-producing drug, but at the same time this does not exculpate it.

It remains to be decided whether in fact society needs yet another intoxicant with possible acute long-term effects, albeit of a social variety. Clearly it is the vulnerable – the young, the immature, and even the merely feckless – who need to be protected from the possible consequences of using intoxicants of any sort. There seems basic good sense in this. Even though cannabis is more freely available in the Western world than it used to be, and although its use may be less harmful than was previously supposed, one cannot just shrug aside the apparent evidence of deleterious effects found in countries where usage has been widespread. Perhaps it should also be said that whilst these ill-effects may not be defined as clearly as many could wish, neither, for that matter, are its supposed good effects. And it is no good arguing that because the widespread use of an illicit substance makes nonsense of the law, that law should therefore be dropped completely. It does seem likely that cannabis may eventually be "legalized," but we should meanwhile make ourselves more aware of the cases for and against it.

Chapter 11

General conclusions

In the previous chapters it was intended to show that indiscriminate use of alcohol or drugs is dangerous. Taken in moderation alcohol is relatively harmless, but uncontrolled drinking produces serious hazards for the individual, his family, and the community. In the case of drugs general opinion maintains that states of dependence are harmful to the individual and ultimately to society. Many would no doubt consider these as understatements, but in the author's opinion the whole area of substance-abuse should rather be the subject of understatements than of extreme assertions.

At the present time a major area of disagreement on the subject has arisen between two elements in society, each of them holding opposing views of the world. One of these groups emphasizes as valuable to the individual a life-style which concentrates on enjoying a wide range of human feelings – often involving rapid and intense changes of experience which may veer from exultation to despair. Their opponents stress the value of self-control, of sober behaviour and the ability to predict and to some extent control alterations in the behaviour of others. It is thus hardly surprising that the conflict between those who value eccentricity and those who value social conformity extends to the area of drug-use.

Perhaps one of the sadder features of contemporary society is that these recognizable types, the conformists and the non-conformists, sometimes seem so intolerant of each other as to wish to exclude each other completely from society. No doubt this basic conflict is largely responsible for the deep-seated attitudes that society displays towards drug-use.

Now medically-trained people may have attitudes towards drug-use which differ in certain respects from those held by members of the police or the probation service; yet on the whole these differing groups are likely to represent the more conformist and "conservative" viewpoint. Their professional activities commit them to a particular standpoint on drugs and their voice is likely to be heard when laws are being made and public policy shaped. This has to be accepted but one might remark that their views will be those on the "right" side of drug-use, so to speak; they are not inherently morally superior to those held by people on the "wrong" side.

People taking an opposite view regard the use of drugs not so much as harmful but rather as potentially harmful, and they believe that the average human being should be allowed to choose for himself how to deal with alcohol and drugs without fear of outside interference. The fact that this view may be eschewed by people with professional experience is not enough to invalidate it. When the situation is carefully considered in the light of present knowledge the effects of drugs that are actually damaging appear to have less to do with the substances themselves and a good deal more to do with the individual using them; that is, they are bound up with his relationships and his environment. This is not to minimize the potential damages of the substances, but merely to try to set them in their true perspective.

Ultimately, there must be some sort of compromise between the extreme points of view. Alcohol and drugs are neither a supreme panacea for man's ills, nor are they inherently evil. If one point stands out it is that extreme attitudes towards the problem are likely to prove harmful. A sense of proportion is badly needed. Idealists and zealots may astound us by their determination, but the stage has been reached in human development where we have outgrown the demands of such extremists and are able to take a more balanced view of man and his behaviour and the world in general. It is unfortunate that over-stated cases are often based on grounds which appeal to the feelings and are not well-founded. The appeal may make itself more alluring by juggling with phrases such as "scientific truth," "the preservation of the nation's morals," or "anarchy and the overthrow of established principles." Nevertheless, the underlying fallacy will remain, and an irrational notion and attitude is passed off under a label that sounds rationally plausible.

An important area of controversy is that concerning the rights and liberties of the individual. Some argue that everyone has the right to take a drug either because he needs to relieve some feeling within himself or because he wants to try out a new experience. Up till now the control of drugs has rested in the hands of medical people, and it has been assumed that individual use of such drugs without medical approval constitutes an abuse. Today many young people say that the use of drugs such as cannabis, amphetamines or LSD is entirely a matter of personal choice, that it is of no concern to *any* medical agency, and that it should be a free and private activity. They support this argument by their observations of the increasing encroachment by the state on the liberty of the individual – and many of us would agree that this encroachment is very real.

We are thus left with a dilemma. No one with any degree of humanity would wish to see further intrusion on the rights of the individual, nor a further erosion of the democratic process. However, society must be made aware of the effects of drugs and the ways in which the use of drugs impinges on the general welfare. It is not unreasonable for the members of our society to exercise a measure of control. In the case of alcohol, still the most widely used and abused of substances, experience has shown that some form of control is needed. In particular, children and adolescents cannot be trusted to handle alcohol safely; it is as obvious as that. Similarly, in the case of many mind-altering drugs, society has a right to expect that they are not freely available to young people. The young are a good deal more vulnerable than older people, and are as open to exploitation by drugs as to exploitation on any other front. Thus it is hard to imagine a good case for the free usage of every conceivable variety of drug.

The next problem concerns the side-effects of drugs. Many of the ill-effects of dependency-producing drugs result from unsterile self-injection, but the various states of psychological dependence are ultimately far more damaging than those of pure physical dependence, for psychological dependence entails grotesque disruptions to the person's way of life. It may well be that too little stress has been placed on the real dangers of psychological dependence, that too much emphasis has been placed on the second-order effects of drug-taking. One need only look at the drugs used in current medical practice. For instance, the development of medicine and psychiatry within the last twenty-five years or even longer has been greatly influenced by the development of the psychotropic drugs. These are drugs which influence mood and mental state and behaviour but without impairing consciousness; they include the major tranquillizers, such as the phenothiazines, and the anti-depressant drugs. The general medical point of view is that these are valuable substances – and so they are when properly used. However, no one would deny that the use of these drugs can be risky and that their side-effects may be severe and even fatal. These side-effects are certainly not to be dismissed lightly. Yet psychotropic drugs are widely prescribed in the Western world. There is even good reason for suspecting that at times they may be over-prescribed, and used unnecessarily. No one denounces such practices, but it could be considere a variety of drug-abuse. For instance, reserpine, one of the earlier-used tranquillizers, was at first said to be exceptionally effective in the treatment of highly-agitated psychotic people. However, it was soon recognized that prolonged medication with this drug could cause profound states of depression and lead to suicide Admittedly there has been a decrease in the use of this drug, but one could logically ask why its use by doctors should be generally regarded as less obnoxious than the use for non-medical purposes of much less harmful drugs, such as cannabis.

To state a dilemma of this kind is not to find a solution. Rather, the purpose is to make people aware of the haphazard way certain drugs are branded as "good" and others as "bad." Such an arbitrar way of making judgements evidently depends on whether the drug is being used in a medical setting, regardless of what its side-effects may be.

The doctor who prescribes a powerful drug must weigh up the possible risks, and in general doctors do assess these sensibly. Accepting a calculated risk is of course part of the fabric of professional training. However, when drugs are taken in a non-medical setting we tend to assume that the person may not have assessed the risk. Yet how far are we justified in this supposition? The risks to health from smoking are well documented, but so far no one has interfered with the individual's right to smoke. The immense hazards to life involved in motor-cycling are obvious, yet no laws are passed against the riding of motor-cycles. The catalogue of risks that are regarded as acceptable in human behaviour is large. Pursuits like skin-diving, parachute-jumping and mountain-climbing are recognized by the bulk of the population as dangerous. Nevertheless these exploits are regarded as valid expressions of human endeavour in the face of certain hazards. When people in such situations get into difficulties, as for example when pot-holers are trapped many hundreds of feet below the ground, or mountaineers get lost on a mountain, there is usually a considerable mobilization of human effort to rescue them – and with justification. Even so, people might question the logic of such rescue operations since the victims knowingly accepted the risk beforehand. When drugs are involved this very argument is often employed. It is said "Well he knew the risk and chose to take it, so why should we help him?" This is not to suggest that drug-taking, rock-climbing or pot-holing are inherently immoral, but merely to stress the fact that when people do take risks the community tends to consider such risks and their consequences by different standards and without resorting to reasonable and logical thought. But then people are neither wholly rational nor wholly reasonable.

References

Advisory Committee on Drug Dependence 1968. *Cannabis.* HMSO, London
Advisory Committee on Drug Dependence 1970. *Amphetamines and L.S.D.* HMSO, London.
ANDREASSON, R., 1962: *Alcohol and Road Traffic: an international survey of the discussions.* Proceedings of the Third International Conference on Alcohol and Road Traffic. London.
BAILEY, M. B., HABERMAN, P. W., ALSKNE, H. J., 1965: *Quart. J. Stud. Alcohol,* 26–19.
BALES, R. R., 1946: "Cultural differences in rates of alcoholism." *Quart. J. Stud. Alcohol,* 6, 480.
BATCHELOR, I. R. C., 1954: "Alcoholism and attempted suicide." *J. Ment Sci.,* 100, 451.
BEWLEY, T. H., 1966: "Recent changes in patterns of drug dependence in the U.K." *Bull. Narcot.,* 28, 1.
BEWLEY, T. H., BEN ARIE, O., JAMES, I. P., 1968: "Morbidity and mortality from heroin dependence." *BMJ,* 1, 725.
BEWLEY, T. H., 1970: "An introduction to drug dependence." *Brit. J. Hosp. Med.,* 4, 150.
BRILL, H., HIROSE, T., 1969: "The rise and fall of a methamphetamine epidemic: Japan 1945–1955." *Seminars in Psychiatry,* 1, 179.
BROTMAN, R., FREEDMAN, A. M., 1965: "Continuities and Discontinuities in the Process of Patient Care for Narcotic Addicts – Final Report to the Health Research Council." New York Medical College.
CHEIN, I., GERARD, D. L., LEE, R. S., ROSENFELD, E., 1964: "Narcotics, Delinquency and Social Policy – the road to H." Tavistock, London.
CHEIN, I., 1965: "Narcotics use as a Personal and Social Problem" in *Narcotics.* 7. Ed. by Wilner, D. M., Kassebaum, G. G. McGraw-Hill, New York.
CHOPRA, G. S., 1969: "Man and Marijuana." *Int. Journal. Add., 4,* 215.
CISIN, I., CAHALAN, D., 1966: *Social Research Project: National Survey of Drinking.* UCLA Symposium.
CLOWARD, R. A., OHLIN, L. E., 1960: *Delinquency and Opportunity: a Theory of Delinquent Gangs.* Free Press of Glencoe, New York.
COCKETT, R., 1971: *Drug Abuse and Personality in Young Offenders.* Butterworth, London.
CONNELL, P. H., 1958: *Amphetamine Psychosis.* Maudsley Monographs. Chapman and Hall, London.

CONNELL, K. H., 1965: "Ether Drinking in Ulster." *Quart. J. Stud. Alcohol,* 26, 629.
CONNELL, P. H., 1969: "Drug Dependence in Great Britain: A Challenge to the Practice of Medicine." In *The Scientific Basis of Drug Dependence.* London, Churchill.
CONNELL, P. H., 1970: "Treatment of Narcotic and non-Narcotic Drug Dependence," in *Modern Trends in Drug Dependence and Alcoholism.* Butterworth, London.
CRUZ, COKE, R., VARELA, A., 1965: "Colour blindness and alcohol addiction." *Lancet,* 2, 1348.
CRUZ, COKE, R., VARELA, A., 1966: "Inheritance of Alcoholism." *Lancet,* 2, 1282.
D'ALARCON, R., 1969: *Bull. Narcot.,* 21, 17.
D'ALARCON, R., RATHOD, N. H., 1967: "Prevalance and early detection of heroin use." *Brit. Med. J.,* 62, 549.
DIETHELM, O., 1955: *Aetiology of Chronic Alcoholism.* Thomas. Springfield, Illinois.
FIELDS, A., TARARIN, P. A., 1970: "Opium in China." *Brit. J. Addict.,* 64, 371.
GERARD, D. L., KORNETSKY, C., 1955: "Adolescent Opiate Addiction: Study of control and addict subjects." *Psychiat. Quart.,* 29, 457.
GILLESPIE, D., GLATT, M. M., HILLS, D. R., PITTMAN, D. J., 1967: "Drug dependence and abuse in England." *Brit. J. Addict.* 62, 155
GLATT, M. M., PITTMAN, D. J., GILLESPIE, D. G., HILLS, D. R., 1967: *The Drug Scene in Great Britain.* London: Edward Arnold.
GLATT, M. M., 1970: "Alcoholism and drug dependence amongst Jews." *Brit. J. Addict.,* 64, 297.
GOFFMAN, E., 1968: *Asylums – Essays on the Social Situations of Mental Patients and Other Inmates.* London. Penguin Books.
GOFFMAN, E., 1961: "On the Characteristics of Total Institutions" in *The Prison.* Ed. Cressey, D. R. Holt Reinhart and Winston.
GOLDBERG, L., 1968: "Drug Abuse in Sweden." *Bull. Narcot.,* 20.1.1, and 20.2.9.
GRIMLUND, K., 1963: "Phenacetin and Renal Damage at a Swedish Factory." *Acta Med. Scand. Suppl.,* 405, 1.
HILL, H. E., 1962: "The Social Deviant and Initial Addiction to Narcotics and Alcohol." *Quart. J. Stud. Alcohol,* 23, 563.
HOLLINGSHEAD, A. B., REDLICH, F. C., 1958: *Social Class and Mental Illness.* New York, Wiley.
HORTON, D., 1943: "Function of Alcohol in Primitive Societies." *Quart. J. Stud. Alcohol,* 4, 199.
Indian Hemp Drugs Commission 1894. Report Simla.
JAMES, I. P., 1967: "Suicide and mortality amongst heroin addicts in Britain." *Brit. J. Addict.,* 62, 277.
JAMES, I. P., 1969; "Delinquency and heroin addiction in Britain." *Brit. J. Criminol.,* 9, 108.
JELLINEK, E. M., 1960: *The Disease Concept of Alcoholism.* Hillhouse Press. New Haven Conn.

JELLINEK, E. M., 1962: *In Society Culture and Drinking Patterns.* Ed. Pitt, D. J., Snyder, C. R., Wiley, New York.
JOYCE, C. R. B., 1970: "Cannabis." *Brit. J. Hosp. Medicine,* 4, 162.
KESSEL, N., and GROSSMAN, G., 1961: "Suicide in Alcoholics." *Brit. Med. J.,* ii 1671.
KESSEL, N., 1965: "Self Poisoning." *Brit. Med. J.,* 2, 1265.
KOSVINER, A., MITCHESON, M. C., MYERS, K., OGBORNE, A., STIMSON, G. V., ZACUNE, J., EDWARDS, G., 1968: "Heroin Use in a provincial Town." *Lancet,* 1, 1189.
KRUSE, H. D. (Ed.), 1956: *Alcoholism as a Medical Problem.* Hoeber. New York.
LASAGNA, L., VON FELSINGER, J. M., BEECHER, H. K., 1955: "Drug induced mood changes in man." *J. Amer. Med. Ass.,* 157, 1006 and 1113
LEWIN, L., 1930: Phantastica, Narcotil and Stimulating Drugs, London, Kegan Paul.
LINDESMITH, A. R., 1965: "Problems in the Social Psychology of Addiction" in *Narcotics.* Ed. Wilner, D., Kassebaum, G. G. 8, 118, McGraw-Hill, New York.
LINDESMITH, A. R., 1956: "Problems and implications of Drug Addiction and Related Behaviour" in *Emerging Problems in Social Psychology.* The Univ. of Oklahoma Lectures in Social Psychology. Series III. 249. Inst. of Group Relations. Univ. of Oklahoma, Norman Oklahoma.
LINDESMITH, A. R., 1947: *Opiate Addiction.* Principia Press of Trinity University, San Antonio, Texas.
LITTLE, W., 1969: "Drug Abuse and Court Intervention." *Int. J. Addict.,* 4, 493.
McCORD, W., McCORD, J., 1960: *Origins of Alcoholism.* Tavistock, London.
MITCHESON, M., DAVIDSON, J., HAWKS, D. V., HITCHENS, L., MALONE, S., 1970: *Lancet* 1, 606.
MOSS, M. C., BERESFORD DAVIES, E., 1967: *A Survey of Alcoholism in an English County.* St. Ann's Press.
MOWRER, H. R., MOWRER, E. R., 1945: "Ecological and Familial Factors associated with Inebriety." *Quart. J. Stud. Alcohol.,* 6, 36.
MULFORD, H. A., MILLER, D. E., 1960: "Drinking in Iowa, II. The extent of drinking and selected socio-cultural categories." *Quart. J. Stud. Alcohol.* 21, 26.
PLYMAR, W., 1955: "The relation of alcohol to Highway Accidents." Alcohol and Road Traffic. Proceedings of the Second International Conference of Alcohol and Road Traffic.
PREBLE, E., CASEY, J. J., 1969: "Taking care of business – the heroin user's life on the street." *Int. J. Addict.,* 4, 1.
RINGEL, E., ROTTER, H., 1957: "The problem of attempted suicide during intoxication." Wien, Z. Nervenheilk., *13, 406.*
RUBINGTON, E., 1967: "Durg Addiction as a Deviant Career." *Int. J. Addict.,* 1, 3.
SAARENHEMO, E., 1952: "Sociological studies on suicides." *Alkoholik Ysynys.,* 20, 5.

SCHUR, E. M., 1963: *Narcotic Addiction in Britain and America.* London, Tavistock.
SCOTT, T. D., WILCOX, D. R. C., 1965: "Delinquency and the Amphetamines". *Brit. J. Addict.*, 61, 1.
SNYDER, C. R., 1958: Alcohol and the Jews: A cultural study of Drinking and Sobriety. Rutgers Center of Alcohol Studies. Monograph No. 1. New Brunswick, N. J. Rutgers Center of Alcohol Studies Publication Division.
SPEAR, H. B., 1969: "The Growth of Heroin Addiction in the United Kingdom." *Brit. J. Addict.*, 64, 245.
TERRY, C. E., PELLENS, M., 1928: *The Opium Problem.* The Committee on Drug Addiction with the Bureau of Social Hygiene Inc. New York.
ULLMMAN, A. D., 1952: "The psychological mechanism of alcohol addiction." *Quart. J. Stud. Alcohol.*, 13, 602.
VATUK, V. P., VATUK, S. J., 1967: "Chatorpan: A Culturally Defined Form of Addiction in North India." *Int. J. Addict.*, 2, 103.
WEST, D. J., 1969: *The Young Offender.* London, Penguin Books.
WIKLER, A., 1952: "Mechanisms of action of drugs that modify personality function." *Amer. J. Psychiat.*, 108, 590.
WIKLER, A., 1952: "A Psychodynamic Study of a Patient during self-regulated re-addiction to Morphine." *Psychiat. Quart.*, 26, 270.
WIKLER, A., 1962: MARTIN, W. R., PESCOR, F. T., EADES, C. G. "Factors regulating oral consumption of Etonitazene solution by Morphine addicted rats." *Pharmacologist*, 4, 154.
WILLIS, J. H., 1969: "The Natural History of Drug Dependence: some comparative observations on United Kingdom and United States subjects," in *Scientific Basis of Drug Dependence.* Ed. Steinberg. London, Churchill.
WILLIS, J. H., 1969: "Drug Dependence: some demographic and psychiatric aspects in U.K. and U.S. subjects." *Brit. J. Addict.*, 64, 135.
WILLIS, J. H., 1971: "Delinquency and Drug Dependence in the United Kingdom and the United States." *Brit. J. Addict.*, 66, 235.
WINICK, C., 1962: "Maturing out of Narcotic Addiction." *Bull. Narcot.*, 14, 1.
WINICK, C., 1965: "Epidemiology of Narcotics Use" in *Narcotics.* Eds. Wilner, D. M., Kassebaum, G. G., 1, 13. New York, McGraw-Hill.
YOLLES, S. F., 1970: "The Narcotic Rehabilitation Act of 1966 and its implications. In Modern Trends in Drug Dependence and Alcoholism." 6. Butterworths, London.
ZACUNE, J., MITCHESON, M., MALONE, S., 1969: "Heroin Use in a Provincial Town – one year later." *Int. J. Addict.*, 4, 557.

Books for further reading

Canadian Government's Commission of Inquiry, *Interim Report.* Penguin 1971

Cockett, R. *Drug Abuse and Personality in Young Offenders.* Butterworth 1972

Cohen, S. *Drugs of Hallucination.* Paladin 1970

de Quincey, Thomas. *Confessions of an English Opium Eater.* Dent 1960

Fisher, R. & Christie, G. *A Dictionary of Drugs.* Paladin 1971

Grinspoon, L. *Marijuana Considered.* Bantam 1972

Hayter, A. *Opium and the Creative Imagination.* Faber and Faber 1968

Huxley, A. *The Doors of Perception.* Chatto & Windus 1968

Jones, H. *Alcoholic Addiction.* Tavistock 1963

Kessel, N. & Walton, H. *Alcoholism.* Penguin 1965

Laurie, P. *Drugs.* Penguin 1967

Leech, K. & Jordan, B. *Drugs for Young People: Their Use and Misuse.* Religious Education Press 1967

Longmate, N. *The Waterdrinkers.* Hamish Hamilton 1968

Louria, D. *The Drug Scene.* Corgi 1970

Lucia, S. P. (Ed.) *Alcohol and Civilization.* McGraw-Hill 1963

Solomon, D. *The Marijuana Papers.* Panther 1969

Willis, J. *Drug Dependence.* Faber and Faber 1969

Young, J. *The Drugtakers.* MacGibbon and Kee 1971

Zacune, J. & Hensman, C. Drugs, *Alcohol and Tobacco in Britain.* Heinemann 1971

Index